GIRL ON FIRE

How to Choose Yourself, Burn the Rule Book, and Blaze Your Own Trail in Life and Business

CARA ALWILL

GIRL ON FIRE

Cover design by Samantha Hauger
ISBN-13: 978-0-578-37571-7

For more, visit www.TheChampagneDiet.com
or email Info@TheChampagneDiet.com

passionista PUBLISHING

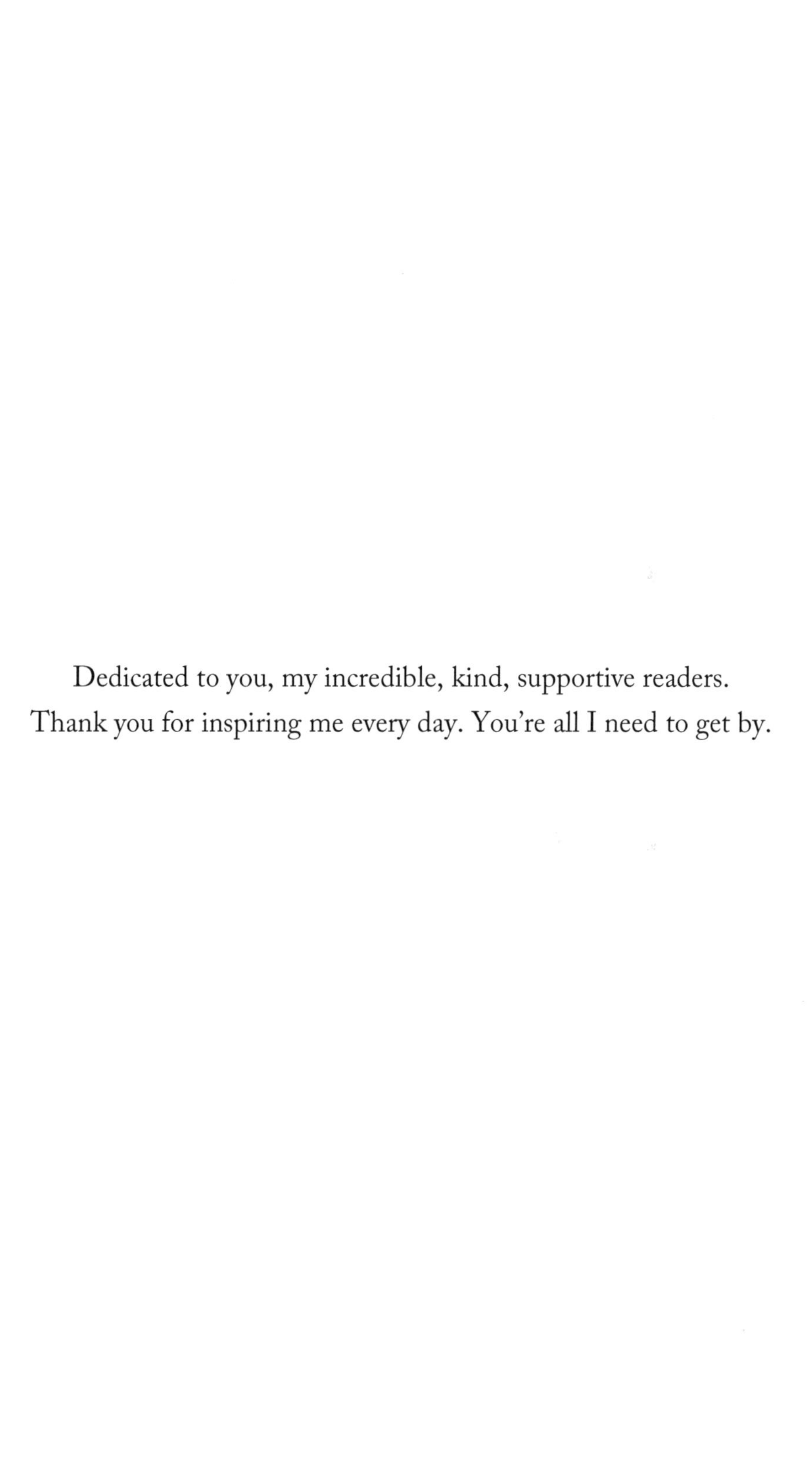

Dedicated to you, my incredible, kind, supportive readers.
Thank you for inspiring me every day. You're all I need to get by.

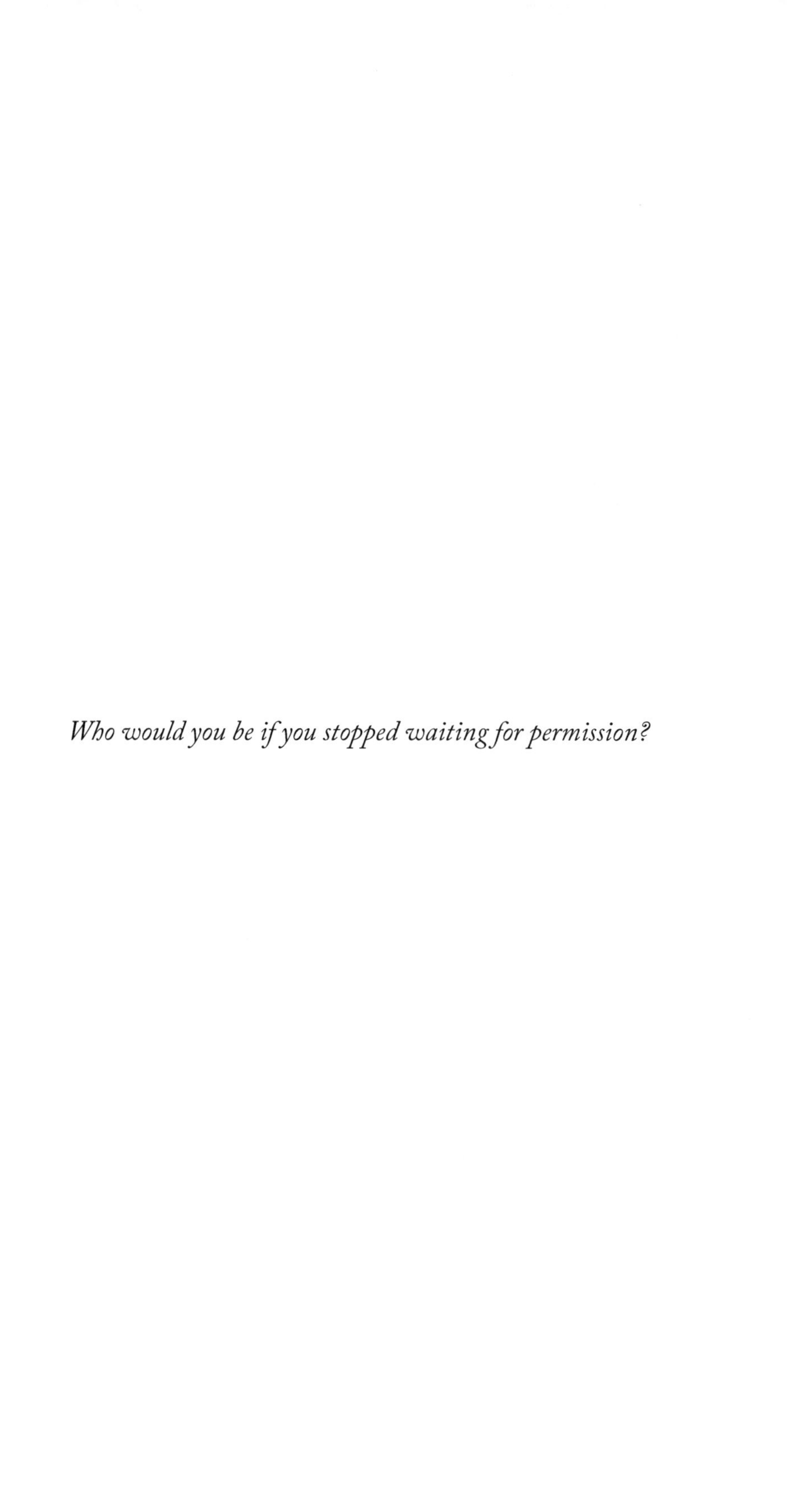

Who would you be if you stopped waiting for permission?

A NOTE FROM THE AUTHOR

In 2015, I self-published a book called *Girl Code*. It was a manifesto for female entrepreneurs who wanted to learn how to break the habit of comparison, trust their own brilliance, and boldly step out into the world to pursue their dreams. A curated collection of my own personal experience and perspective as an entrepreneur, peppered with standout advice from other women in business, and packed with actionable exercises to move you toward creating your own future, *Girl Code* became a worldwide sensation, transcending cultures, age groups, and industries. The book launched a movement of women who learned it is not just important to support other women in business – it is necessary. In fact, it was such a hit that Penguin Random House decided to offer me a book deal to re-publish it and take the message even further. To date, *Girl Code* has now been translated in seven languages.

Four years after its original publication, I'm still receiving dozens of messages per day from women across the globe who are discovering the tenets of *Girl Code*, and using the book to transform their lives and businesses. One of the most powerful messages I recently received was from a woman who discovered an unauthorized, underground translation of the book in her local library in Iran. She shared with me that *Girl Code* gave her hope, and most importantly, the push to pursue her dreams of becoming a musician in a country where women face more adversity than most of us can imagine. I didn't even care that someone had translated the book without my approval, or that I wasn't making a dollar from it. None of that mattered to me when I realized my book was helping these women who just wanted to be happy in a society where they are often left powerless and diminished.

When I shared an image of that unauthorized version of the book on my Instagram account, more and more Iranian women messaged me to share that they, too, had discovered *Girl Code* and were so grateful for its message. I can recall at one point in time, thinking that landing on the *New York Times* bestseller list would be my pinnacle of success as an author someday, but the letters from these Iranian women – and all women from around the world – have blown that idea out of the water. To think that a body of work I created and self-published from my dining room table in my small, Brooklyn apartment is changing the narrative of a culture is a gift I can't quite put into words. And to me, *that* is what true success looks like.

It was that message, and the thousands of others I have received throughout the past few years, that have propelled me to write this much-desired follow up to *Girl Code*. Now that women entrepreneurs are banding together in sisterhood and realizing the importance of collaboration over competition, it's time to take things to the next level. It's time to rise up, together, and challenge the status quo. It's time to question the way things have been done in the past, to write our own rules, and do life and business *our* way. The world needs us to utilize our voices now more than ever. We must step into our power and we must let nothing hold us back.

The business world is changing rapidly, and there has never been a better time to choose yourself. Gone are the days of waiting to be chosen by an agent, a record label, a company, or a publisher. We no longer need the gatekeepers, we just need an unshakeable belief in ourselves and an unstoppable drive to make it happen. You'll notice I decided to choose myself for this book, and self-publish once again. There's good reason for it. And we're digging into all of it.

Now is the time to show up for ourselves. We all have the ability to design a career beyond our wildest imaginations without permission, selection, or validation. *Girl on Fire* will show you how to do it.

This book is for every woman who has had a vision that others might not understand. It's for every woman who is sick and tired of playing by the rules. It's for every woman who has known she was meant for more and has waited far too long for someone to give her the permission she thought she needed.

I'm so thrilled you have decided to join me for this conversation. Let's do this.

With love,

CONTENTS

INTRODUCTION **1**

PART ONE – CHOOSE YOURSELF **5**

Chapter 1 – Choose Yourself 7

Chapter 2 – Stop Waiting for the Title and Crown Yourself 23

Chapter 3 – View Rejection as Redirection 33

Chapter 4 – Speak It into Existence 39

PART TWO – BREAK THE RULES **49**

Chapter 5 – Don't Be Afraid to Be the Full Package 51

Chapter 6 – Generous Girls Go Further 61

Chapter 7 – The Power of You 69

Chapter 8 – Competing Leaves You Powerless 79

Chapter 9 – There is Room for You at The Table 89

PART THREE – BLAZE YOUR OWN TRAIL **95**

Chapter 10 – It's Never Late to Be Who You Secretly Dream of Being 97

Chapter 11 – The Beauty in Being a Best-Case Scenario Girl 107

Chapter 12 – What Are You Available For? 117

Chapter 13 – You Can't be a Victim and a Success at the Same Time 125

Chapter 14 – Why Not You? 133

INTRODUCTION

When I sat down to write this book, I asked myself: who is the woman who needs no permission? Who is the woman who chooses herself, who waits for no one, and who blazes her own trail in life and in business? Who is the *Girl on Fire*?

In the world of business, there are enough blueprints for success floating around out there to make your head spin. There are coaches and self-proclaimed experts and network marketing uplines and #girlbosses who all seem to have their own formula for success. At any moment of the day, someone is on Instagram or a podcast or a Zoom call declaring that *they* have the secret sauce. Just pay 12 installments of $5,995 and you, too, can do it all *just like them.*

When people talk about industries being saturated, it's only because everyone is out there trying to be a carbon copy of everyone else. Of course, it doesn't feel like there's room for anyone else when every single business looks identical to the next! How could there be?

In a crowded marketplace, potential customers and clients don't need another copycat – they need *you.* The real you. The raw you. The rule-breaking you. The you that knows exactly who she is, and what she wants. The innovative you. The creative you. The you that doesn't need a permission slip to put herself out there and chase all of her dreams. The you that sets the world on fire just by being yourself.

It's time to break out of those boxes we've been squeezing ourselves inside of. It's time to reject the status quo, become intimate with our own intuition, and start doing things *our* way. It's time to step into our uniqueness and be bold enough to choose ourselves, burn that damn rule book, and step into our power as capable, talented, badass women.

It's time for a revolution.

I decided to create a "*Girl on Fire* Manifesto" to set the tone for this book. Who is the woman who chooses herself? Who is the woman who just goes for it? How does she think? How does she work with others? What's important to her? What are her values? These points below will guide you on your journey, and we'll unfold each one in detail throughout the following chapters. I recommend bookmarking this page, because you'll want to come back to this often and use these as quick reminders when you need a little boost.

The *Girl on Fire* Manifesto

She chooses herself. She doesn't wait to be chosen by the gatekeepers or celebrated by the mainstream.

She is her own permission slip, and she needs no approval. She isn't consumed with what people say about her, and she doesn't wait to pursue her dreams until she has enough "likes" online, or in real life.

She views rejection as redirection. She strives to evolve, not give up. She takes constructive criticism and creates magic with it. She doesn't spend time feeling bad for herself. She is in a constant state of refinement and growth.

She speaks kindly to herself and optimistically about her dreams. She chooses her words wisely and creates a mental environment of positivity and hope.

She rejects the status quo. Just because something worked in the past doesn't mean it's the only way to do things. She comes up with creative solutions and thinks outside the box. She does business in a way that *feels* good. Her metric for success is how on fire she feels while she's creating.

She knows failure is a possibility but she does it anyway. She values experience over winning. She's addicted to the feeling of not knowing what is going to happen next. She knows that without rejection, there is no chance to reinvent herself.

She knows generosity is a growth strategy – the more she gives the more she gets. She is fulfilled by helping others and lifting them up. She is focused on impact before income, and she knows that when she is generous with her time, her content, and her energy, it comes back to her tenfold.

She proudly celebrates her success. She knows that by shining her own light, she creates space for other women to do the same.

She creates strong boundaries to protect her energy and peace. She is intentional about who has access to her, and she spends her time wisely. She would rather channel her energy into changing the world than comparing herself to strangers on social media.

She doesn't want to reach everyone, she wants to reach *someone*. She doesn't have to be the biggest or most well-known. She doesn't care about shallow fame or celebrity. She wants to make an impact.

She doesn't want to play "the game." She knows the system is rigged and she gracefully bows out. Instead, she blazes her own trail and lights her own way. And as a result, the world can't keep their eyes off of her.

PART ONE:

CHOOSE YOURSELF

CHAPTER ONE

CHOOSE YOURSELF

Have you ever found yourself obsessively refreshing your email, impatiently waiting for some HR manager to tell you that you've been chosen for that new job? Or maybe you know exactly what it feels like to look at your phone 27 times in one hour to find out if that publisher you sent your manuscript to is going to offer you a book deal. Or perhaps, you find yourself checking your Instagram dozens of times per day, praying your post gets enough likes for you to feel validated in your work. Whatever the desperate case, one thing is certain: it sucks to wait for someone to choose you.

I can recall so many moments in my own career where I've put my fate in the hands of a gatekeeper. You may recall my publishing story from my book *Girl Code*. If you haven't heard the story, or you want a quick refresher, here it goes. It was the Spring of 2011, and I was working my full-time, soul-sucking job in digital advertising at MTV. Working for MTV may sound glamorous to some, but the reality was, I was trafficking ads on the internet for ten hours a day, bored, burnt out, and in desperate need of a change.

I had been writing my blog, *The Champagne Diet,* for three years at that point. I had always dreamed of writing a book, in fact, that was my impetus for starting my blog in the first place. By 2011, I knew that the cubicle life was a life I could no longer live. I wanted more. I decided it was time to get serious about my publishing dreams and plan my escape from Corporate America.

It should be noted that I had zero friends who were authors, let alone any friends who had even attempted to write a book at that point. Anyone I shared my dreams with was somewhat supportive but made sure to warn me that making a living as an author is next to impossible. Isn't it interesting how people who have never done what you want to do are quick to shoot down your dreams? Here's a tip: don't take advice from anyone whose shoes you wouldn't want to be in.

I didn't know any editors, agents, or publishers either, so it was on me to figure out what to do to make my book writing dreams a reality. I went on a massive Google rampage, digging into every author-friendly rabbit hole I could find during my downtime at work. I'd sit at my cubicle, day in and day out, waiting for a few free minutes so I could obsessively Google "How to publish a book." That search took on many new forms as I gathered more and more information. Some included, "How to get a literary agent", once I discovered this was the first step to landing a traditional book deal, which at the time, I thought was my only option.

Then, I had to figure out "How to write a query letter." This is the way you get in the door with said agent. Months went on and I signed up for online writer's forums, asking strangers on the internet as many questions as I could. Let it be known – the most efficient way to learn something is to look it up on the internet. You don't need friends in high places or mentors when you have a Wi-Fi connection.

I eventually wrote a cringe-worthy query letter that I began sending off to every literary agent I could find online. Looking back at that first email and sample chapter I sent to agents, I have to giggle. As Reid Hoffman said, "If you're not embarrassed by the first version of your product, you've launched too late." And I live by the mantra, "You don't have a chance if you don't take a chance," so I took mine. Though I clearly had no idea what I was doing, that query letter was good enough to pique the interest of a few agents who actually replied to me. Considering 96% of query letters get rejected, I was *ecstatic* to have been chosen.

After a few conversations, I wound up signing with a literary agent who I felt understood my vision and believed in my writing. We worked on my book proposal for six, long, anxiety-filled months. Then the time came for her to begin what's called the "submission process." This is where agents introduce your book to editors through your proposal.

I remember the obsessive thoughts that took over my mind during that time. It was right after Thanksgiving, so things were slow at work. I'd sit at my desk, with nothing else to do but stare at my email inbox, willing a message to pop up that my book had sold. I'd imagine all the possible scenarios. Which editors would bite? I took the submission list and followed each editor on Twitter (this was before the days of Instagram, if you can believe it). I read their bios and their tweets and imagined who might like me best. I sat there and waited, and waited, and waited to be chosen.

By the time January 2012 rolled around, nobody had chosen me. In fact, I was rejected by a whopping 19 editors. I'd be lying if I said those rejections didn't sting, but there was no way I was allowing 19 random people to decide my life's path. Maybe they were having a bad day? They didn't know me. And they certainly didn't know my potential. I was going to be an author, and nobody was deciding otherwise.

At that point, I had two options. I could throw in the towel and give up on my dream, or forge ahead and find a different way. Around this time, Seth Godin had published a blog post called "Reject the Tyranny of Being Picked and Pick Yourself." I read the post after fielding all 19 of those publisher rejections and flirting with the idea of self-publishing my first book. At the time, the publishing world was going through a major change. Amazon had completely disrupted the industry by creating a platform for authors to choose themselves and self-publish their own books.

Suddenly, self-published books were coming out that were making major waves. They were as polished and professional as those coming from the antiquated traditional publishing model. In fact, many were better. The stigma of self-publishing was quickly disappearing. Authors were not self-publishing their books because they couldn't land a book deal – they were choosing to self-publish to retain their rights to their work, maintain creative control, and take ownership over their careers as authors. And Amazon was making it easier than ever for them to do so.

Seth's words lit a fire in me. If someone as forward thinking and brilliant as he was didn't need a gatekeeper, why should I? He noted Amanda Hocking's self-published success and how she made a million dollars a year sharing her work on Kindle without a publisher. He mentioned Rebecca Black and her big hit "Friday" (remember that one?) reaching more than 15,000,000 listeners without a record label.

I won't give away the whole blog post, as you can and should Google it yourself, but the point Seth made was that it's a cultural instinct to wait to get picked. And once we reject that impulse, we're suddenly free from the anxiety around waiting for someone to choose us and we can actually get to work. It was just the next-level thinking I needed to help free me from my own craziness and just fucking go for it.

Back to the drawing board (also known as Google University – have you enrolled yet? It's free and *everyone* gets accepted), and back down the rabbit holes I went. Figuring everything out, just me and my keyboard, my fingers typing furiously, learning, asking questions to strangers on the internet again, and collecting information on how to self-publish a book. I wound up utilizing a platform called Createspace, now called KDP. It's Amazon's print-on-demand service that requires no upfront costs. You can literally publish your book for $0, with no overhead costs outside of what you spend on your cover design and your editor, and you get a royalty check each month from your book sales. I paid about $300 for my cover, and about the same for my editor who made sure there were no glaring spelling errors or major grammatical flaws in the book. It was easy, efficient, and fast.

A few months later I had self-published my first book, *Sparkle.* That book did better than I could have imagined; even hitting the #1 spot in a few bestseller categories on Amazon. And I credit that success to the fact that I cleared myself of the need to be chosen and I just chose myself. I was able to work smart and hard, and get myself and my readers excited about the book. I wasn't pre-occupied with what a publisher might be able to do for me. I had to make it happen for myself. And I did.

By 2015, I had self-published a total of three books, all while working my full-time job (I wrote most of them from my cubicle at

MTV). I was doing well with my little side hustle, bringing in anywhere from a couple hundred bucks a month, sometimes even earning $1,000 a month in royalties. And then I self-published *Girl Code.*

One year later, *Girl Code* had sold about 50,000 copies. To put things in perspective, according to *Publishers Weekly*, the average traditionally published book (with a big team, marketing power, and a large budget) sells about 3,000 copies in its lifetime. The average self-published author sells 250 copies or less. And she earns less than $500 total from her books. I had independently sold 50,000 copies of *Girl Code* in a year, beating all the odds. And all of a sudden, a lot more people were taking notice of me. Among those people were many of the publishers who had rejected me a few years earlier.

Don't ask me how *Girl Code* took off the way it did; it was magic. I didn't have an assistant, a team, or a huge budget to promote the book. There was no marketing or launch strategy other than passion and generosity. I was sharing content from the book non-stop to my audience because I believed in it so much. I was so proud of *Girl Code*, and I showed up for myself, day in and day out, both on and offline to prove it. I set up my own events, agreed to speak for free at any event that would have me, and basically became my own promotional machine. I'd hand out the book for free at events. I'd leave copies in back pockets of airplane seats so the next passenger would find it. I'd even write little notes inside the title page, encouraging that person to pass the book on to someone who needed it. Passion and generosity have always been the only strategies I use when it comes to my work. And who can deny a woman driven by those two things?

By the end of 2016, I received an email from an editor at Portfolio Books, an imprint of Penguin Random House, who was interested in working with me. This was the same publisher who published

#GIRLBOSS, and, coincidentally, many of Seth Godin's books. I won't lie – it felt damn good. At that time, I was still working through the need to be chosen. And to be chosen alongside those powerhouse authors? I was pretty proud of myself. Although I had already given myself permission to be an author, and as successful as *Girl Code* had been, there was still a longing inside me to have that traditional publishing experience. It was a dream I still felt like I had to explore.

I accepted the offer from Penguin to re-release *Girl Code* and publish my next work, a book called *Like She Owns the Place.* I had done well in self-publishing, and now I wanted to know what it was like to have a team behind me. It wasn't an easy decision to partner with a publisher, after realizing the power of my own brand and success, but I felt like I had to follow through on a lifelong dream and take a chance.

"What happens when your dreams come true and you don't recognize them?" my SoulCycle instructor and dear friend, Noa Shaw, asked our class one sweaty summer afternoon as we climbed a hill to a U2 song. I suddenly felt my face turn beet red and I burst into tears. Right there, in the middle of my spin class, I found myself sobbing into an over-bleached white towel, trying to stop myself from crying my eyelash extensions off. I don't remember the rest of what he said, but that question alone brought up all the emotions inside of me that had been building during the launch of *Like She Owns the Place*, the first book I had written under a publishing contract. I was emotionally exhausted, filled with anxiety, and not happy.

Before I go on, I'd like you to know that I do not regret working with my publisher on that book. I'm forever grateful I got to have that experience. I also don't want it to sound like I'm trash-talking them, either. I know they did their best, but the traditional publishing model ultimately let me down. And I'm laying it all out here because I need you to understand the full picture. There were some upsides, like getting more distribution for my books in book stores and airports, foreign language translations, and getting to work with a talented editor.

There were also challenges. I was now working with a large team, and not everyone was on the same page as me. It wasn't easy to trust others with my vision when I had been on my own for so long. I had disagreements over various aspects of the marketing and promotional efforts for the book. I had certain expectations that were not met. The process took far too long for me (you're looking at your book being released 12-18 months once you sign a book deal, and I don't really *do* patience). Even though I had a team, I actually felt more alone than ever. In fact, I felt more depressed during that entire experience than I had in years. I gained close to twenty pounds, I lost my motivation, and I missed being an indie author.

From the outside looking in, I'm sure nobody would believe, or even understand why I felt this way. I finally had that book deal! I was able to live off a large, six-figure advance and write all day. I was now aligned with the big names in publishing. From the outside looking in, I was living the dream. But in reality, I was miserable. When you're a forward-thinking entrepreneur at the core, it can be frustrating to work with people, systems, and models that are outdated. I felt like I had gone backwards. I felt held back.

Through all the highs and lows of my traditional publishing experience, I learned one major lesson. And now that I'm able to connect the dots looking backward, I know this lesson came for a reason.

I learned that a book deal did not validate my success as an author. And it did not give me anything I couldn't give myself.

Your success as an entrepreneur in any business endeavor is entirely dependent on you. It has nothing to do with who you are aligned with or acknowledged by. And that became even more apparent to me during the launch of *Like She Owns the Place,* where my role as an author did not become any easier with a team behind me. Sure, a publisher may be able to get you an opportunity or two, but ultimately, your success depends on your willingness to step up to the plate, do your best work, and make things happen for yourself. You are required to fill the gaps where things aren't being done, and show up for yourself.

After realizing that I wasn't going to magically be splashed across the *New York Times* or thrown a huge book launch party filled with tastemakers just because I now had a publisher, I got down to business. I started creating opportunities for myself, the way I always had for all those years before I had anyone backing me up. I reached out to every female leader, blogger, and podcast host I could think of. I wound up connecting with dozens of underground influencers and speaking to large groups of women about the book. I appeared on any podcast that would have me. I just wanted to reach as many women as possible with my message in a powerful and authentic way.

I set up nearly fifty interviews by myself over the course of two weeks during the launch of *Like She Owns the Place,* far more than my publisher did for me. I stayed up late and woke up early so I could be available to multiple time zones. I often ate dinner at my desk (which was more often than not a few glasses of wine and a block of cheese…don't judge me). I set up giveaways and signed advance copies to send out to anyone willing to pitch in and share the book on social media. I coordinated my own book launch party. My friend, Gwen, who is an incredible publicist and a great friend, wrote a press release for me and generously emailed it to everyone she knew at the magazines and websites that aligned most with my brand.

I assumed the role of author, marketer, intern, assistant – all of it. And the truth is, any successful business woman will tell you she's done the same. Of course, it's important to ask for help, and to delegate where we can, but in order to be truly successful, you can't ever be above a task that will help move your business forward. Find me in the post office on the regular, wiping down tables before an event, and emailing out invoices to clients when I need to. Because ultimately, nobody will care for your business the way you do.

By the way, it's important to note that I chose myself again for this book. After *Like She Owns the Place*, I broke away from my publisher, and decided to go back to self-publishing. If that's not a full-circle moment, I don't know what is.

To date, I have earned over half a million dollars self-publishing my own books, and that number continues to grow each month. That's a far cry from the statistic I shared earlier about the average self-published author earning less than $500 from her books. And it's all because I decided to *choose myself.* My success is not an anomaly either. It is available to anyone who wants it. You've just got to be willing to put in the work, and cast aside the belief that someone needs to choose you. You've got to be willing to expand your faith in yourself and get out there and make it happen.

Successful entrepreneurs don't wait for their "big break" – they create it. They don't wait to be featured in a magazine, or picked up by a publisher, or given a chance to speak on a stage. They promote themselves on platforms they create, they self-publish their own books, they launch their own podcasts, they create their own events and build their own stages.

Beyond the financial success of my self-published endeavors, what's even more meaningful to me is the impact my books have had on women. I received a message a few days ago from one of my readers who told me that she is a suicide survivor, and that my words now give her purpose. You cannot put a dollar amount on that kind of impact. And frankly, a publisher doesn't care about that. They care about your ability to make them money. So, are you going to wait around to be chosen by an organization who is focused purely on financial success? Or are you going to get out there, fearlessly put your art out into the world, and potentially change someone's life? I think that one's a no-brainer.

By the way, if you're thinking about writing a book and still unsure about which direction to go in, allow me to share some of the realities of working with a traditional publisher:

They retain the rights to your work.

It takes 12–18 months on average to publish your book. The truth is, you and your audience can't afford to wait that long.

They have final say in the creative process.

They keep the lion's share of the royalties.

They do not throw you a book launch party, or cover the cost of any events supporting your launch.

Their marketing and PR efforts are minimal.

Just another reason to choose yourself in business, as opposed to waiting for those gatekeepers to choose you. Nobody is going to work as hard for you as you will for yourself. And that is a fact.

Do you ever notice that the opportunities so many of us dream of are the ones where someone else is in charge? We put our success in external outcomes; in being chosen. We anxiously wait for someone to publish us, verify our Instagram account, feature us in a magazine, or give us some kind of public acknowledgement of our hard work. And when it finally happens, we're left wondering why we don't feel the way we thought we would when we imagined it in our minds. Our dreams come true – and we don't recognize them.

What is it about being chosen that comforts us? Why do we wait to be selected and aligned with someone in perceived "power" to feel like we're suddenly good enough? And why do we assume those people we desperately want to choose us have any power anyway?

For many of us, the fear of rejection rules our choices. When I self-published my first book, I was terrified of being ripped apart by book reviewers. In fact, it's what kept me stuck for so long. I clung to the idea of finding a publisher because I imagined myself being mocked all over Amazon with no one else to validate me. I felt like if I had a publisher, the bad reviews might be less of a blow because "at least I was chosen." At least I'd be "a real author."

When I finally decided to choose myself and put my book out there, without anyone backing me up, it wasn't half as scary as I had imagined. Of course, there were a few crappy reviews, but that's life. And I'll tell you what – having a book deal can't stop those bad reviews anyway. You've got to build up a belief in yourself so strong that someone's opinion of you doesn't become your reality.

James Altucher said, "When we are not chosen, we feel bad. When we are chosen – even by idiots – we feel good. We need to unlearn this imprisonment. Not dissect and analyze it. Just completely unlearn it." I urge you to think about an area of your career where you find yourself waiting for selection or permission. What part of you still needs to feel validated? What part of you still needs to feel chosen?

Then ask yourself: Who would I be if I stopped waiting? What would I put out into the world if I didn't need permission? Who would I be if I just fucking went for it?

In the space below, write down something you've been waiting for permission to do in your business:

____

____

____

____

____

How has waiting served you?

____

____

____

____

____

How would your business change if you stopped waiting for permission?

____

____

____

____

____

KEY TAKEAWAYS + NOTES

KEY TAKEAWAYS + NOTES

CHAPTER TWO

STOP WAITING FOR THE TITLE AND CROWN YOURSELF

I want you to think about a dream you have that feels a little too big for you right now. For example, while I was waiting for a publisher to pick up my book, I didn't *feel* like an author. I thought being chosen would give me that feeling. I didn't even realize I had the ability to crown myself as an author all along. Nobody had more power to give myself that title, than myself.

Before you can be fully comfortable choosing yourself, we need to work on banishing the limiting beliefs that may be holding you back. If you were 100% confident in your abilities, you would have probably chosen yourself already. It's okay if you're not! That's what I'm here for. You may need that extra push to let go of the fear or judgment, believe in your abilities, and finally write yourself the permission slip you think you need.

I was chatting with one of the riders in my spin class the other day. She's a comedian and she really wants to write a book about her life. I asked her what's stopping her, and she said she keeps asking herself, "Who am I to write a book?" I asked her if she had stories to tell. She said, “Yes.” Then I told her, “Great! You’re an author. Now start writing.”

What she, and many women experience, is something called Imposter Syndrome. It is defined as “A psychological phenomenon in which people are unable to internalize their accomplishments” and according to research, it affects women more than men. It’s especially common among successful women. Imposter Syndrome is a nagging feeling that one day you may be exposed as a “fraud” or outed for not being good enough to do what you do. My former client and friend, business coach Jamie King, has a brilliant exercise to snap yourself out of this mindset. She encourages her clients to think about what it would actually look like if an imposter were to step into their shoes. If you feel like a fraud for writing a book about your life, imagine if someone who didn’t know you, and had zero experience in your life tried to tell your story? *That’s* a fraud. You’re not an imposter for evolving and trying something new.

Imposter syndrome still affects me, even after everything I’ve accomplished. And I think it’s important to share that with you. I’ve just learned how to dismantle it and move through it quicker. I’ve written, re-written, re-arranged, and changed my mind about this book for well over a year. I have struggled with self-doubt, writer’s block, anxiety, lack of motivation, and a whole other host of feelings. I have wondered if anyone still cares about what I have to say, if my best work is behind me, or if I have anything left to say at all. All of those feelings are normal, and part of the creative process. If you’ve ever felt the same, you’re not alone.

But you also aren’t powerless.

The fastest way to plow through self-doubt is with action. When I struggled with writer’s block, I sat down at the computer every day and wrote anyway – even if it sucked and I wound up re-writing it all. When I worried if my best work was in my past, I moved forward regardless and kept creating new work. Despite my fears, I am an author. I crowned myself years ago, and I remind myself of my power daily. And it's time for you to do the same.

Sometimes, we create stories about why something is out of reach for us. Let's talk about my friend, Jamie, again for a moment. I just returned home from speaking at *The Summit of Slay*, a massive event she held for hundreds of women entrepreneurs in Louisville, Kentucky. I remember when Jamie first told me about her vision for the event a few months back. She had never hosted anything like this before, and she had no idea what she was doing. Yet, she dove in head first, learned along the way, and she killed it! It was honestly the best event I have ever spoken at or attended – and everyone who was there agreed.

When we got home, Jamie sent me a message that she's ready to finally start writing her book, *Attention Whore*, that she's been talking about for years now. I told her how excited I was for her, and she responded, "But why is it so hard to start?" I said, "Because you're telling yourself it's so hard." I just watched this woman create magic. Her entire event went off without a hitch and she changed hundreds of lives for the better. I know she's capable of writing a damn good book. But somewhere along the way, she told herself it's hard. The only hard part about writing a book is convincing yourself it's not.

It's time to proudly and confidently step into the new version of yourself right now. It's time to decide you are completely capable. It's time to crown yourself. Got it?

Let's walk through the steps it takes to make that happen.

If you're thinking about launching a blog, let's say, I want you to immediately start referring to yourself as a blogger. Then, take an action step, today, to make that dream a reality. Whether it's launching your website, or writing your very first post. You are now a blogger, sister! When you crown yourself, you begin taking actions that align with that title. Quick tip: the sooner you can move, the sooner it starts to feel real.

I have a lot of friends and clients who are coaches for a major health and fitness network marketing company. Many of them began their journeys as customers, falling in love with the products and programs and achieving their own personal success before deciding to help others. One of the most common threads among these women when launching their businesses was that they couldn't mentally move from customer to coach. As a coach, they were now responsible for running a business. They couldn't call themselves an entrepreneur. They were waiting to hit a certain rank in the company, or bring in a certain amount of money in their business. They were waiting to be acknowledged by someone – anyone – else.

The truth is, the sooner you can acknowledge *yourself*, the sooner you will achieve the success you desire. Nobody is responsible for crowning you. You must fearlessly and confidently chase your goals, and step into the next-level version of you – no matter how many customers you have, how much money you are making, or how much validation you're getting from the outside.

I know it sounds easier than it actually is. I understand; it actually took me years to call myself an author without cringing, even after I had self-published three books! We have some serious programming to undo in order to truly break through and blaze our own trails without the fake safety net we think we need.

Let's start by breaking down some of the limiting beliefs that hold us back.

I'm not good enough. In my experience, this is the number one reason women hold themselves back. They're convinced that they aren't good enough, fit enough, smart enough, or skilled enough to do what they want to do. The truth is, there are people out there with less talent, and less experience than you, crushing it. Why? *Because they decided to start.* You get better as time goes on. Acquire the basic skills you need to get started on your path with some level of confidence, and then let go of the "perfectionist mindset" and get to work.

It's not the right time. Zig Ziglar once said, "If you wait for all the lights to turn green, you'll never leave your driveway." There is never a "perfect" time to begin any new adventure. You become more and more equipped for the journey while you're on it. That's where you pick up speed. If I had waited until I felt the time was "right" to self-publish, I would not be here today, writing my ninth book. If I had waited for permission from a publisher to write my book, I'd never have written anything at all. Whenever I tell someone I've already published eight books, I'm met with an audible gasp and a "OMG! How did you do that?"

I started. That's it. Simply put – I did the work.

The best way to dismantle the belief that it's "not the right time" is to set a goal with a timeline for yourself. For example, "I will start promoting my new business by X date" – and then stick to it. Hold yourself accountable to your goal and know that there will never be a better time than right now. How else do you think I got my ninth book out there?

What if I fail? I want you to think about a woman out there who is killing it right now in her business – someone who inspires you daily. Imagine if she never got started because she was afraid she might fail? My friend, Noa, often reminds me to stop thinking thoughts that scare me. We can choose to focus on all the things that can go wrong, but what if we started to imagine everything that could go right? Life changes when we let optimism rule. We'll dig more into this idea later on in this book.

The next time the fear of failure pops into your head, flip that thought on its head. Start fantasizing about what success would look and feel like for you. Close your eyes, and create an elaborate movie scene in your mind's eye. Visualize, in detail, what life would be like if you achieved your dreams. What would you be doing? What would you be wearing? Where would you be working and living? When we create positive thoughts, the negative ones run out of space and can no longer thrive. Repeat this practice whenever the scary thoughts creep in. And think about those women you admire who gave themselves permission to do to the same.

I don't have the money. This is a crappy, outdated excuse, babe. And I refuse to allow you to accept it. The truth is, you need a lot less than you think. With all of the tools we have access to right now, like the internet and social media, it's easier, and more affordable than ever to launch your business. Self-publishing costs zero dollars. There is absolutely no investment to get your book up on Amazon. Of course, I recommend hiring an editor and a graphic designer to create a great book cover for you, but those things can be done on a budget, and sometimes you can even find a friend to do it for you.

Maybe your dream is to launch a clothing store. It may be a stretch to rent a space right now, but you can certainly run it online, for free, from your social media page. Start by investing in a few pieces, and then when those pieces sell, put that money right back into your business. Use sites like Fiverr to find someone to create a cheap logo for you, or better yet, use a program like PicMonkey to make one yourself. I made my own logo for my online boutique, Dagmar Rose Vintage. It's a free font on a black background. And it cost me zero dollars.

Promise me that you will let go of the idea that you need a ton of money to get started. The best things truly do come from humble beginnings. A simple idea. A blog post. A Facebook group. Do you know my friend RaeShanda Lias-Lockhart began a Facebook page in 2011 called *All is Fair in Love and Fashion* where she helped women style themselves based on what was in their closets? She gave advice every day to help women create new looks with the clothing they already owned and reinvent themselves through fashion. RaeShanda now owns a six-figure boutique business by the same name that continues to expand every year. She was also a teen mom of twins, homeless, and an army veteran, so I won't take your excuses. This powerhouse is one of the most inspiring women I have ever had the pleasure of meeting. She is an example of what it looks like to put your past behind you and decide that you are worth every single thing you desire. I suggest looking her up and reading some interviews she's done. Or better yet, go see her speak in person. She'll change your life.

You're the only one who holds limiting beliefs about yourself and what you are capable of achieving. I can promise you that. We're our own harshest critics, and all that criticism does is keep us stuck. If you've felt any of the above, use the space below to blow up those beliefs by replacing them with a positive action you'll take.

For example, "I'm not good enough" turns into "I am enough and today I will write my first post announcing my new business venture."

____

____

____

____

____

KEY TAKEAWAYS + NOTES

KEY TAKEAWAYS + NOTES

CHAPTER THREE

VIEW REJECTION AS REDIRECTION

Every woman who chooses herself has experienced some sort of rejection in her past. And rejection leaves clues. The brightest women don't just steamroll past the "No's" – instead, they search for value inside of them. They ask themselves, where can I refine my product? How can I improve my skills? Do I need to pivot? Is there an opportunity here to grow? Can I handle this differently next time?

It's important to have an open mind and realize that when you are rejected, you are just being redirected. And suddenly, you have the gift of time. You can take a step back, assess the situation, and find a new creative solution. When my first book was rejected by all those publishers, I asked my agent for feedback from each one. I wanted to know why they didn't want me. I wasn't afraid of being hurt, and I wasn't pitying myself – I wanted the feedback so I could grow. I took that time and used it to evolve.

Once I heard the common threads, I got to work. I looked for areas to improve my writing so that when I self-published, that book would be better than ever. I took a memoir writing course to learn how to better tell my personal stories. I made some changes to my manuscript. And most importantly, I became intimate with the real decision makers – my future readers. I took that time to share excerpts of my book with my audience to get their feedback. I realized I essentially had a giant focus group that I could now tap into, and their feedback was more valuable than any publisher's. By sharing my content with them, I was providing value, and I was also gauging their interest in specific topics that I had planned to write about. Some ideas were better received than others, and the ideas that knocked it out of the park made it into that book.

When we are rejected, we also get to ask ourselves the million-dollar question: why did I want to be chosen so badly anyway? Rejection is a crash course in self-awareness. We get a chance to become intimate with our own intuition. We get to dive deep and more often than not, realize that we never needed that person/organization/ gatekeeper to validate us in the first place.

If you've ever been rejected, here are a few ways to move forward in a positive and productive way:

Keep building. One of the critiques I received from publishers back in 2011 was that I didn't have a big enough platform. So, I made it my business to keep building my platform and put myself in a position where nobody would ever determine my worth based on a metric like that again. I took to Twitter, Facebook, and then Instagram once it started gaining popularity. I showed up every single day, providing my audience with value and asking nothing in return. My goal was simply to connect. I viewed my rejection as a blessing, because I realized I had complete creative control over my content. I didn't have anyone looking over my shoulder, telling me how or what to post.

If you've been rejected, keep building your platform. Get out there in front of as many people as possible. Offer to speak at events for free. Show up in the places where you want to be seen. Make your voice louder. I pitched a local newspaper in Brooklyn back in 2011, and they showed up at an event I held at a bookstore to promote my blog before my book was even out there. Their coverage of *The Champagne Diet* went viral and led to articles in *Glamour*, *Shape*, *MSN Australia*, and even *The Daily Mail* in the UK. This was before I had even self-published! You never know who's watching you. But you've got to keep showing up in order for anyone to see you.

If you're climbing the corporate ladder and you've been turned down for positions, continue to build your skill set. Take courses, connect with people in the spaces you want to be in, and make yourself known. Gain the confidence you may be lacking by immersing yourself in everything you need to know about your dream job. Get so good that the next time around, you don't even need to interview for that role – you're sought out for it.

Analyze how you handle rejection. Do you freak out? Shut down? Get defensive? Use it as further proof to back up your tired story of "I'll never make it!"? Or do you search for the greater meaning? Do you handle it with grace? Rejection is a crash course in self-awareness. How we show up in these moments is everything. I was hurt when I was rejected, and sometimes, I still am. That's totally normal. But I move through rejection much quicker now. I look for the clues, find the value in the "No", and I keep going. I use it as fuel to get better. I know that I am my own permission slip, and nobody's opinion of me holds more power than my own.

Connect the dots looking backward. As Steve Jobs once said, "You can't connect the dots looking forward; you can only connect them looking backwards. So you have to trust that the dots will somehow connect in your future." If I had gotten my book deal in 2011, I wouldn't have had the experiences that have shaped me into the woman I am today. I would never know the depths of my own power, or the ability to determine my own path. I would never have had the chance to give myself permission to publish my own books. In retrospect, I can see that rejection as one of the best things that has ever happened to me.

View your rejection as redirection. Turn the place you've landed into the best place you've ever been.

Think of an area in your career where you've faced rejection. How can you reframe it? How can you allow that rejection to serve you?

____

____

____

____

____

KEY TAKEAWAYS + NOTES

KEY TAKEAWAYS + NOTES

CHAPTER FOUR

SPEAK IT INTO EXISTENCE

Have you ever wondered why things just seem to always work out for some women? They always get exactly whatever they set their sights on, they're eternally optimistic, and it looks as though they never really struggle. Do they work hard? Sure. But these babes aren't available for exhaustive, fearful hustle.

Well, I've got some great news for you – we can *all* be that woman.

The way you speak about your dreams is one of the most powerful forces in the universe. Your success is not dependent on who you know, how much money you have, or dumb luck. Your success is completely dependent on your *self-belief*. And if you're constantly talking about how things never work out for you, or how you don't have what it takes, that's what the universe is hearing. And as a result, that's exactly what your reality becomes.

I've mentioned my online vintage boutique, Dagmar Rose, in previous chapters. Here's how it began. I've always loved vintage fashion, but never gave much thought to starting a business around it. I had always dreamed of one day owning some kind of clothing boutique, but I never really had a clear vision for it, so I kept that dream on the back burner. Until one October afternoon, when my cousin Nicole called me and asked if I wanted to join her for a weekend course at The Fashion Institute of Technology (FIT). We both love fashion, and the course was all about vintage. I said yes, thinking we'd make a day of it, learn a few things and go to lunch. I had no idea I'd decide to start my own vintage business by the time we sat down to order appetizers at that lunch.

The course turned out to be magical – better than I could have ever anticipated. What inspired me the most was our teacher – she was in her mid-sixties, decked out in head-to-toe vintage, full of life, and so passionate about the topic; and, as a result, I found myself feeling instantly passionate as well. It was like she brought something out of me that had been dormant for a while. After the first session, she brought the class out on a shopping excursion. We went to flea markets and thrift stores around New York City and I wound up finding some of the most unique pieces I've ever seen. My shopping bags were filled to the brim with vintage jewelry, coats, and accessories that I had scored for great prices.

Before we go on, you should know, I've *never* been a haggler. In fact, I avoid the sale racks in big department stores because they give me major anxiety. All those crazy women swarming around, elbowing each other to snag that size medium white silk blouse for 70% off? No, thanks. But there is something about the thrifting process that is so exhilarating to me. Finding that amazing, rare item, like a needle in a haystack, negotiating a lower price with the seller, and then taking it home, breathing new life into it, styling it, and re-selling it became my new addiction quickly. Phew! My heart races just thinking about it.

But back to my story.

So, Nicole and I go to lunch that afternoon after our class, and I tell her I'm going to start an online vintage boutique. She's supportive, of course, but she definitely thinks I'm a bit crazy, as most people do when I go full-force with a new idea so quickly (it's kind of my thing). I go home, order a slew of books on Amazon, and begin obsessively researching the fashion vintage industry. I watch interview after interview with successful vintage store owners on YouTube. I take more courses. I don't know a soul in the business, but I work my ass off to educate myself and gather as much information as I can online. I basically make these store owners my secret mentors. They don't know me, obviously, but I observe them from afar and take notes. If you've ever wanted to learn something and felt like you needed a mentor, find one online. You don't need an in-person mentor, in fact, I have never had one. Everyone who has taught me something has done it from afar. They never even knew I existed.

I order garment racks and jewelry displays and transform my home office into a mini store. I start thrifting a few times a week and building my collection. I decide to name my shop Dagmar Rose Vintage, after my grandmother, who inspired my love for vintage in the first place. I begin photographing, styling, and selling items right from my Instagram page. Every day, I'd take a pic and post a cute caption, letting my followers know "this item will go fast!" The reality was, I didn't know how fast the item would go, but I had a gut instinct and I decided I would only speak positively about my new passion. If I believed the item would sell (which I did), then it would! And guess what? Every time I shared something, it sold out immediately. My inbox was flooded with messages from women asking me how they could get their hands on my next piece because every time they tried to buy something, it was gone.

I continued to enthusiastically post my pieces and share the brand-building process in my daily Instagram stories. I went all in on this new business. And as a result, it became incredibly successful – and it continues to grow and bring me so much joy.

I could have launched Dagmar Rose Vintage with an entirely different mindset. I could have gone into the business with fear, anxiety, and self-doubt looming. I could have talked to everyone I knew about how nervous I was, how I didn't have the time for it, and what a risk it was to invest money into something that could possibly fail. I could have apologized to my social media followers for evolving my brand and sharing something new. But all of that uncertainty would have been shared into the universe, and I would have received uncertainty right back. I would not have found the success that I did, and the entire process would have sucked the life out of me, rather than give me energy. Instead, I chose to give myself permission to follow a dream. And it was one of the best decisions I've ever made.

It's incredibly important to speak our dreams into existence. That means speaking positively and optimistically about the things we want, and talking about them with certainty that they will happen. Of course, we must do the work, but the way we speak about our dreams is crucial to their success. We must believe, beyond a shadow of a doubt, that we will experience good things that help drive our vision forward. We must believe that the right people will show up, at the right time, and guide us on our journeys. We must believe that we will be successful, and we must be bold enough to say it out loud.

It's not enough to just think it, or use creative visualization or journaling. Those tools are important, but the words we speak hold the most weight when it comes to achieving our goals. Without positive, affirming words, our dreams stay within the confines of our mind. But when we start speaking about our success, we plant the seeds of positivity in the minds of those around us. Confidence is contagious, and if you believe in what you're doing, others will, too.

Something clicks when we speak positively about our dreams. We begin moving toward them with confident action. We don't consider doubt, because it doesn't exist any longer. We create our new reality. And that reality is filled with optimism, faith, and momentum. Does this mean everything is going to work out perfectly right off the bat? Not necessarily. But we'll get to that later. For now, I want you to get into the habit of positive thoughts, positive words, and positive actions.

Here are a few tips on how you can begin speaking your dreams into existence, and using your words wisely:

Turn your doubts into confidence. Rather than speak about what might not work, speak about what is currently working. For example, you might be tempted to say, "How will I ever be successful in such a flooded industry?" But you're working toward your goals for a reason. You have *some* belief in yourself, so let's amplify that. Take something positive about what you do and speak about it confidently. For example, "I'm going to rock this, because I know I bring X to the table." Even if you've failed in the past, you are here, and you are thriving. Everything is a lesson, and when you realize you're exactly where you're meant to be, it's easy to see your life as a gift.

Speak with trust. This might be one of the most challenging things you do, but when you nail this, everything changes. You should speak with a sense of knowing and trust, as if you have a crystal ball and you already found out your dream will turn into a reality. This is called certainty. And when you realize the domino effect of its power, you will become a manifesting machine. For example, I talk about my future brick and mortar store constantly. I even have a Spotify playlist with the music I'll play in there, and I have a signature candle scent picked out! I am certain that my store is on its way to me. I trust that I will get what I want. I release the control of the "when" and the "how" and I keep following my intuition and working toward what I want. If you're skeptical of this technique, then I want you to ask yourself, how will doing the opposite serve me?

Don't indulge the dream killers. Be cautious of those who tell you to "be more realistic." I call these people the dream killers. For whatever reason, they have a negative mindset about dreaming. They never give themselves permission to do the things they want to do, and they have a hard time relating to women who do. They'll find every single thing that could go wrong with your dreams, and warn you about all of them. It's just better to bite your tongue around these people, and find people who are positive and optimistic like you to share your deepest desires with. If you feel alone, find a Facebook group with like-minded women, or, even better, find a local group of women on MeetUp.com. I've met some incredible people through Meet Up and I know a lot of women who have as well.

The more you talk about it, the more people can help you. It just makes sense, doesn't it? If you keep everything inside, there is no opportunity for people to step in and help you. When you share your dreams with the right people, they can offer assistance. And people love to help! You'd be surprised at how many people can make an introduction for you, open a door for you, or even give you a new idea to help propel you forward.

What is one dream that you'd like to speak more positively about?

____

____

____

____

____

____

____

Up to this point, what have you told yourself about why this dream might not become your reality?

____

____

____

____

____

____

____

How can you reframe that conversation? What positive things can you say about your dream?

KEY TAKEAWAYS + NOTES

KEY TAKEAWAYS + NOTES

PART TWO:

BREAK THE RULES

CHAPTER FIVE

DON'T BE AFRAID TO BE THE FULL PACKAGE

Have you ever felt like you wanted to do all the things, *and* create a business or career out of all of them? Have you ever been nervous to try something new because some of some antiquated advice from some "expert" about "staying in your lane?"

My mom loves to tell a story about when I was in pre-kindergarten. One afternoon during pick up, the teacher asked to speak with her. "Cara's a very bright girl, but she doesn't listen to instructions," the teacher explained. Concerned, my mother asked what was going on. The teacher held up a piece of paper where I had drawn hearts around all of the answers to a quiz where we were asked to identify all the words that started with the letter "B", rather than circles. Every single answer was right, but the teacher marked me wrong because I didn't draw circles as we had been told. I chose to draw hearts around my answers. Apparently, I was in the mood to do it my way. And not much has changed! My mother defended me, but the teacher wasn't budging. She refused to look at the fact that I had actually scored perfectly on the exercise. She was too caught up in the rules.

That kind of conditioning starts at a young age and continues throughout our entire lives. Once school begins, we're taught to fall in line, to hinder our own self-expression, and to do everything like everyone else – or else. Then we become adults, and those rules expand into jobs where there's little room for play. We're given dress codes and handbooks and instructions. We're then given performance reviews based on how well we follow those codes and rules. It's no wonder we're terrified to trust our intuition and do anything differently!

Now don't get me wrong. I understand that as a society, we need some kind of order. We can't be running amuck from childhood, without ever being taught about morals and the fact that we should probably wear pants in public. But there's a fine line between keeping order and completely stifling people's creativity and self-expression and stuffing them into boxes.

As a business woman who has done many things and done them successfully, I'm here to dispel the myth that you must play by the rules to be successful. In fact, quite the opposite is true. Think about the great women in history who changed the world: Rosa Parks, Mother Theresa, Ruth Bader Ginsberg, Anne Frank, Madonna, and Malala Yousafzai, to name a few. Whether they made music or they made noise, one thing is for sure – they all pushed boundaries and they did things their way. And they all had a massive positive impact on our culture. As Laurel Thatcher Ulrich said, "Well-behaved women seldom make history."

So when it comes to your career, please know that you do not have to pick one thing and stick with it forever. You can – and should – give yourself permission to explore whatever lights you up. Take it from me: a bestselling author of eight books and counting, a business mentor, a clothing designer, a podcast host, a professional certified master life coach, a vintage fashion boutique owner, a speaker, and a woman who created many other streams of revenue in her business. I even dabbled in health and wellness coaching at one point during my own personal journey. I even had an entire corporate career before all of this. And who knows what will come next? I get excited just thinking about all the possibilities.

It is completely possible to shift, pivot, and do whatever it is that you want to do. You don't need to stay in your lane. You need to create your own lane, and thrive in it.

In my opinion, the most interesting women are the ones who are multi-passionate. They recognize all of their talents, and they know they don't belong inside of a box. I recently discovered a powerhouse of a woman on Instagram and her bio listed: DJ, TV Personality, Boutique Owner, Bodybuilder, Speaker. I was drawn to her instantly and spent a good fifteen minutes on her page learning everything about her. I signed up for her email list and I can't wait to know more about her. She sounds fabulous, daring, and interested in life.

So many women are terrified to try new things because they're worried about looking "all over the place" or they're afraid of what people will think. They're so afraid to break some bullshit business rule, so they hold back their talents, dim their light, and shrink themselves. I'm here to remind you to *stop giving away your power.* Do you really think you were born to do just one thing? Do you really think your God-given talents are that limited? There's more for you, girlfriend. And you're doing yourself – and the world at large – a disservice if you don't let yourself explore it all.

If this resonates with you, and you know you're meant to do more than one thing on this planet, then please hear me out: you were given your gifts for a reason. You're meant to "make a ruckus" as Seth

Godin says. And if you are privileged enough to be able to make multiple contributions to this world, do not take that for granted. We every drop of you. It's time to stop holding back.

So, how do you do it? How do you actually become a multi-dimensional business woman? The secret is in your ability to execute. Pick the things you want to spend your time on, and start executing. Start taking daily actions that help build out those arms and legs of your brand that you feel passionate about creating. This goes for entrepreneurs, as well as corporate women, and those who want to start a "side hustle" and run their business part-time at night or on the weekends. Much like this new woman I just followed on Instagram, who I'm sure got serious about each of those titles listed in her bio, you've got to get serious about your passions if you want to make them a part of your brand. And not everything can make the cut.

Prioritize your passions. As Oprah Winfrey once said, "You can have it all, just not all at once." I recommend getting a pen and paper, and making two lists. Your first list should include all the things you currently love doing, and the things you'd love to start doing someday.

Then, start a second list. This is the list that includes the things you know you actually want to take action on in the near future. The things on this list should excite you and make you feel ready to *move.*

For example, maybe your first list includes designing clothing. You've always loved fashion, and one day you'd really love to start designing and manufacturing your own dress line. But when you break down what it takes to actually go out and do that, you don't feel ready for it. That's okay! That's how you strategize and get serious about your execution.

Maybe that first list also includes writing your first book. That decision feels good to you, and most importantly, it feels like something you can and will take action on now. You move it over to the second list, and then start creating daily actions to drive you forward to that goal, like writing for twenty minutes each morning.

The secret to doing the things you truly want to do is in your execution.

Focus on what lights you up, not what others expect of you. When I decided to launch Dagmar Rose Vintage, I will admit, I was a little nervous about how it might be received by my audience. I've always been known as someone who shares inspiration and advice, especially to women entrepreneurs. Would anyone actually care about vintage sequin jackets? Let alone want to buy one from me? I could have either leaned into my fears, or leaned into my execution. I decided to bury the self-doubt and focus on my passion. I got moving. And my vintage business is booming. It has also inspired me to share more fashion-related content, like shopping hauls, styling tips, and advice for women who want to feel more glamorous.

If I've learned one thing, it's that when you have passion, you cannot fail. I don't think every single one of my followers loved my pivot to fashion, but that didn't stop me. In fact, I know some people unfollowed me. I also gained a ton of new followers who appreciate what I'm doing. And a lot of my followers stayed, even though they weren't into the fashion posts, just because they appreciated seeing me go after a new dream.

But does your social media following really matter anyway when you're feeling good about your choices? Your happiness is more important than your follower count. Remember that. At the end of the day, *I* loved my pivot. And most importantly, I'm evolving my skill set, I'm creatively challenged, my bank account is overflowing, and I'm having a ball. And that's what matters most.

Following your passions makes you more interesting. Here's something else to consider: your audience knows when you're not into something anymore. They can sense when you aren't feeling it, or you're just doing something because it's profitable. They know when your heart isn't there. I couldn't spend the rest of my life *only* sharing life or business advice based on my past experiences. I would have been bored to tears telling the same stories over and over again. I had no choice but to give myself permission to evolve and explore all of my obsessions, and I am so happy that I did.

Launching a new business gave me an opportunity to expand my faith in myself. I had a whole new set of fears to face, and a whole new set of experiences to pull inspiration from. And I've used each one of those experiences to empower my audience in a brand-new way.

These days, I share a mix of everything: fashion, life advice, business tips, fitness inspiration, or whatever I'm loving at the moment. But one thing remains: I'm not scared to be myself. And you shouldn't be either.

Remember: you get to choose the woman you want to be. You get to make the rules. You get to have it all, in a way that feels good to you. You *can* have a dynamic, creative, interesting business without feeling overwhelmed. You can stand out in the crowd and *wow* your clients by following your obsessions in a strategic and inspired way. Figure out what you want to do most, and follow those things up with execution. Be consistent and lean into your passion. The right audience will resonate with you, and your business – and your spirit – will flourish.

What's something new you've been dying to explore and possibly bring into your business or career? Write it down in the space below:

What holds you back from doing this?

What would it take for you to just go for it?

What positive things will come out of you diversifying your brand?

KEY TAKEAWAYS + NOTES

KEY TAKEAWAYS + NOTES

CHAPTER SIX

GENEROUS GIRLS GO FURTHER

The other day, I got a message from a woman from Pakistan who was unable to buy my book *Girl Code*. She wasn't asking me for anything, just expressing her frustration because she really wanted to read it and couldn't find it in her country. "Send me an email and I'll send you a free digital copy," I replied. She was so excited, and she emailed me a few minutes later and I sent her the e-book version of *Girl Code* so she could read it on her computer.

The next day, I posted an image on Instagram with a screen shot of my email to her and a caption inviting anyone who wants to read my books but is in a country where they don't have access to them to email me, and I'd send them a free digital copy. The comments section was flooded with people who were so surprised and happy that I was doing such a thing. But why wouldn't I? I want every single woman in the world to have access to learning and empowerment, and that should not be determined by which platforms or book stores decide to carry my books. So if that means losing a few dollars that I would have made on an e-book, who cares?

In fact, every few months, I run free book promotions on Amazon where anyone can access my e-books for free (I would offer the paperback version, but I'm limited based on what Amazon allows me to offer). I've had people tell me that they can't believe I'd "lose money" like that or they seem so shocked that I'd be willing to give away my books for free. I don't see it like that at all. I see incredible value in what I do. I've seen casual readers turn into superfans. I've seen college students and single mothers who are literally living on their last dollar so grateful that they were able to finally read my book that was on their Amazon wish list for months. My goal is always impact before income, and generosity has taken me further in my life and career than a quick sale ever has.

It feels damn good to be kind, and that is worth more than any royalty check I could ever receive. And if you're doing it in a genuine and authentic way, it is also the best business strategy you could ever employ if you want to stand out and stick around.

In Gary Vaynerchuck's book, *The Thank You Economy*, he stresses the importance of developing strong, honest, interpersonal relationships with our customers and clients in business. He writes, "I want people who love running businesses and building businesses as much as I do – whether they're entrepreneurs, run a small business, or work for a Fortune 100 company – to understand what early adopters like me can already see – that we have entered a new era in which developing strong consumer relationships is pivotal to a brand or company's success. We have been pushing our message for too many decades. It's no longer enough that a strong marketing initiative simply funnels a brand's one-way message down the consumer's throat. To have an impact, it will have to inspire an emotionally charged interaction."

Gary walks his walk. You'll see him regularly answering hundreds of tweets a week, replying to comments online, and spending hours engaging with his audience. And he admits getting yelled at by his friends who are high-powered CEOs who think it's a waste of time. Gary's response is that depth is far more interesting than width, in a world where width has become obnoxiously loud and impossible to break through. I recently watched a video where he talked about a large order that came in for his wine company. A man bought a $111 case of Pinot Grigio. Gary decided to find him on Twitter, and he noticed the man was non-stop tweeting Jay Cutler, the former quarterback of the Chicago Bears. Tweets like, "Jay Cutler I love you. Jay Cutler I'm mad at you. Jay Cutler you're the best." Clearly, this guy was a fan. Gary called his office and instructed one of his team members to go on eBay and find a signed Jay Cutler jersey and send it to this man. The jersey was $350, much more than the 8% profit he made on that wine, but the point was to show appreciation, and make an impact. By going out of his way to generously thank his customer, Gary not only made that man feel amazing and appreciated, but he feels amazing himself.

He also knows it will come back to him. In fact, it did. That man wound up sharing the story with a friend, who wound up ordering $4800 worth of high-end red burgundy.

In a world where every marketing and sales "expert" is instructing us to constantly engage in money-making activities or else we're wasting our time, I find mine and Gary's approach to be a breath of fresh air. Almost any business coach will tell you that you should constantly be thinking about how to turn someone into a customer. They'll have you creating funnels and "free 7-day challenges" and opt-ins that always lead people down a road where – surprise! – the next step is to buy your program or product. Here's the thing: every single marketer is doing this and every single potential customer is onto you. They may opt in for a while to see what they can get for free, but chances are, they're going to opt out the minute they feel like they're being sold to.

It's time to focus on generosity, relationship building, and actual connection first. People are human beings. They are souls. They aren't payment plans or followers or dollars in your bank account. Gary says, "You have to scale the unscalable if you want to break through the noise today" and he is absolutely right. It takes patience and an ability to hold a long-term vision for your business, but it's worth it if you plan on sticking around for a while.

This doesn't mean you shouldn't ever share your offers with your audience. But you've got to have relationships with those people before you can ever expect them to spend money with you. And it has to happen organically – not in the form of another blueprint or strategy.

To help develop strong relationships with your customers or clients, I recommend getting in front of people as often as you can, in real life, to really drive this point home. Host a meet up and meet your social media followers in person. Go to an event and connect with the people there. Have a drink with them. Go to lunch. Have a genuine conversation and learn about their lives and their dreams and what's important to them. And most importantly – remember why you do what you do. More than likely, you didn't start your business simply to make sales. You started because you wanted to solve a problem; to make people's lives better. Allow yourself to be led by that, and remember that generosity leads to more abundance and magic than you could ever imagine.

Write down your generosity plan. How can you show up without expectation and serve your audience?

____

____

____

____

____

KEY TAKEAWAYS + NOTES

KEY TAKEAWAYS + NOTES

CHAPTER SEVEN

THE POWER OF YOU

A few years ago, I was approached by a large corporation to speak at their yearly summit. They wanted me to be their keynote speaker and share my message with thousands of their attendees. It would have been an incredible opportunity to get my book *Girl Code*, which was newly released, in front of a massive group of women. After a conversation about what I felt I could bring to the table, and what they were looking for, I shared my speaking fee: $10,000 plus first-class travel. They were game.

A few days later, I received another phone call, expressing their concern with some of my "language." They still wanted me to speak, but as a super conservative organization, they asked that I curb my cursing. That even included the word "damn."

Damn.

I was completely taken aback. I told them I'd need to think about it. I don't exactly have a potty mouth, but I certainly don't hold my tongue if I want to drop an F-bomb here or there. I'm a passionate New Yorker, and sometimes the stronger language just fits. Sometimes "fuck" just feels appropriate.

After a few days, I decided that I could not stand on a stage and be preoccupied with the anxiety of making sure I avoided specific words to tell my story. It would have been completely inauthentic for me to change who I am at the core - even if I was going to make $10,000 for less than one hour of work.

So, I turned down the gig.

Walking away from that opportunity was one of the most empowering things I've done in my business. I can't say many people would have done the same. But my personal brand is my most valuable asset. And it should be yours, too.

Giving yourself permission to *be* yourself is a game-changer in life and in business. And being yourself is essentially what a personal brand is. Women who blaze their own trails have strong personal brands, and it flows effortlessly because they don't hold back. They recognize the power in what makes them unique, they double down on their strengths, and they are proud to share themselves the world. They don't become chameleons or change their beliefs to fit in.

When helping women get clear on their personal brands, I like to ask them a few questions: What do you stand for? What's important to you? What kind of people do you want to work with? What are your non-negotiables? Who are you at the core?

Do you feel clear on what *your* personal brand is? If you're unsure, you are not alone. I'm here to break it down for you and help you realize it's easier than you think to identify yours and start integrating it into your work. You don't need to pay an expensive coach or spend thousands of dollars on a website makeover, either.

Your personal brand travels with you through life no matter what your career is. You have a personal brand as an entrepreneur, as a stay at home mom, as a corporate professional, or as a barista at Starbucks.

Your brand is evident in the way you dress, in the way you speak, in the way you make others feel. Your personal brand is the style in which you do life. It is your truest essence. It's something that will evolve as you evolve. You have a personal brand whether or not you realize it, so you might as well take control of it. It's time to get intentional about the way you show up in the world.

I recently spoke at the Massachusetts Conference for Women on this very topic. The audience was mainly corporate professionals, many of whom were in the tech industry. Most of these women had never given much thought to their personal brand at all, and I can't say I blame them. When I worked at my corporate job at MTV, personal branding wasn't much of a conversation. Everyone was so focused on doing their job, because that's what we were ranked by and rewarded for. Of course, personal relationships were important, but everything was secondary to our daily duties. We certainly weren't *choosing ourselves.*

Speaking to that roomful of corporate women and answering very valid questions about curating your personal brand in the workplace reminded me of the common and current challenges that arise when women in all types of careers face this task. Questions came up like, how do I figure out what my brand is? How do I promote myself without feeling gross? How do I share my wins with my boss in a respectful way? These questions apply to women who work in all settings, whether that's running your own online business, working a corporate job, running a network marketing business, or owning a brick and mortar.

Let's begin with you. What makes you, *you*? What makes you unique? What do you love to do on the weekends? What music do you listen to? What is your ultimate dream? Favorite food? Identifying the rich layers that you possess as a dynamic woman are key in cultivating your personal brand. I want you to think of this as less of a strategy and more of an exploration of the self.

I think that's where the idea of personal branding becomes daunting to some – both corporate professionals and entrepreneurs. We tend to think of this as another job or another "show" to put on, when in reality, the secret to personal branding is just identifying and celebrating more of yourself. Weirdness not just included, but necessary!

Use the space below to write some key things about yourself. For example, "I love '80s music, and my favorite artist is George Michael," (ahem) or, "I make the best banana bread you've ever tasted." Don't hold back. List it all!

____

____

____

____

____

Now that you've begun to curate your personal brand, I want you to start thinking about ways in which you can share it with the world. If you're in a corporate job, think about how you can start talking about the things you love to your co-workers. Maybe you're a foodie, and you're constantly checking out new restaurants in your city. Over morning coffee at your cubicle, strike up a conversation about that new spot you tried, and recommend your favorite dish. Before you know it, I bet those co-workers will start asking you for recommendations on where to go out to eat for date night. They'll begin trusting your judgment and you'll stand out in the office as someone with great taste (literally).

And who knows? Maybe when a new position opens up in another department that you really want to go for, the hiring manger will have heard your name already. "I know Jess! She recommended that fabulous restaurant that I went to with my husband last month." Giving ourselves permission to share our personal brand makes us interesting, impressive, and unique.

If you're an entrepreneur, it's even easier to share the diverse and fascinating things about yourself. You have the incredible advantage of utilizing social media to amplify your business and become more known. Maybe you're a life coach who loves making jewelry. You've been dying to share some of the rings you've made with your audience, but you're worried it might come out of left field. Remember: you create your own rules. The fact that you make jewelry makes you interesting and unique! Don't hide it! Hop on your Instagram story, and share. Take your followers through the process of designing and creating one of your pieces. Talk about how much you love doing it, and what a fulfilling, creative outlet it is for you. I promise, it will blow your audience away and they'll love you even more. And who knows, maybe that passion project will turn into a side hustle that you can monetize? Remember, we can be *money-making multipassionistas!* I'm living proof.

Your personal brand extends beyond your interests. It's also about the way you make others feel. I think this is one of the most overlooked aspects of personal branding. We tend to focus on the self, but if we aren't making others feel good, we're neglecting a major aspect of the way we show up in the world. When people talk about you, they're talking about your brand. If someone has a stellar experience with you, and they rave about you to their friends, that's branding.

Of course, the opposite is true as well. If you're rude to someone, they'll surely share that as well, and again, that reflects your brand. You know that saying, it takes years to build your reputation and seconds to destroy it? It's the truth. Just something to be aware of as you navigate situations. It's just a good look to put your best self forward. Of course, we're all human, but industries are small and people talk. So avoid gossip and drama and treat others as you'd like to be treated. The Golden Rule is the only rule I follow.

A Quick Guide to Shining Your Light (Without Feeling Gross)

The beautiful thing about personal branding that you have complete control over it. And when the good reviews come in, it's on you to share them! A lot of women are nervous to share things about themselves because they don't want to sound like they're self-promoting. You've *got* to get over that, babe. When I get a kind message, or a glowing book review, you can bet I blast that all over the place. I can't expect anyone to assume that my book was great, or that someone had a wonderful interaction with me. I love to share those words because it helps others instill trust in me. And you should be doing the same.

The same goes for my corporate girls. When I was a director at MTV, I encouraged my staff to be proud of their wins. I had a team of twenty people under me, and I loved hearing about their good work. If a client sends you a beautiful letter of appreciation, do not hesitate to forward that e-mail to your boss. You can include a message like, "This made me feel so good, I thought I'd share it with you." Or feel free to toot your own horn during your weekly meeting with your boss. There's a way to do this humbly, without sounding arrogant or off-putting. At the end of the conversation, after your boss has led the meeting and when things are wrapping up, you can add something in like, "I wanted to mention to you that Shane from Proctor & Gamble reached out to me and told me he loved that report I created for him!" Ain't nothing wrong with letting them know. Toot toot!

Your personal brand is also about what's important to you. Have you ever created a personal mission statement? I'm not talking about your business mission statement, either. I'm talking about a personal statement that reflects your purpose in the world. Why are you here? What do you hope to achieve by being on this Earth? This one is a bit heavy, but it's so important. Creating a personal mission statement helps you define your values and get clear on what matters to you as a woman. I recommend doing this yearly, as you grow and evolve. You can even make it part of your New Year routine. I like to do this around January 1st, before I think about my goals. I sit down with a notebook, light a candle, and create an inspiring vibe for myself to get into as I write my personal mission statement. Here's an example of my latest one:

I'm here to empower, uplift, and inspire women around the world. Through leading by example and living my best life, I show others what's possible. I know that everything happens for me, even the challenges. I utilize every lesson to become more self-aware, more compassionate, and more loving. I meet each person on my path with kindness and respect. I am here to make a positive impact and shake up the world in the best way possible.

Now, it's time for you to write your personal mission statement. This is your personal brand:

____

____

____

____

____

KEY TAKEAWAYS + NOTES

KEY TAKEAWAYS + NOTES

CHAPTER EIGHT

COMPETING LEAVES YOU POWERLESS

A few days ago, I was shopping at an indoor flea market in SoHo and I came across *the* most beautiful vintage fashion boutique pop-up. As I approached the shop, I admired the way everything was displayed, from the pink antique carpets, to the way the jewelry was laid out, to the rolling racks of gorgeous clothing. I greeted the woman who was working the shop and complimented her setup. She had her head buried in her phone and barely acknowledged me. I politely asked if I could take a photo of her display because I was so inspired. She raised her head from her phone, looked me up and down, and bluntly said, "No."

Shocked, I asked her why. "It's my policy. I don't want anyone copying me." I explained that everything looked so beautiful and I wanted to share it with my friend, who is an interior designer that often helps me brainstorm ideas for my own spaces. "That's exactly why I don't allow photos. I don't want people seeing what I do and copying it. Tell your friend she can come here and buy something if she wants to see my shop."

After I picked my jaw up off the floor, I very kindly told her, "You know, I respect your decision, but it's really a shame that we can't just all inspire each other. It doesn't need to be a competition." I just couldn't keep my mouth shut, and I was hoping she'd hear me and something might shift within her. She had nothing to say back, and just buried her head back into her phone and continued to ignore me.

That experience stayed with me all day. I actually felt bad for this woman, because I knew she was coming from a place of lack; a fear-based mindset where she truly felt like someone else might gain success by "copying" her ideas. Sadly, this is a common thought process. Competition is an antiquated mindset that many people still cling to in almost all industries. It's actually very forward-thinking to believe that collaborating with your peers is more valuable than competing with them. Unfortunately, many business owners, including that woman, are still stuck on that old school mentality that someone can "steal" their success.

The reality is, despite her fears, nobody can do it like she does. And that's what makes her special. Even if I took a photo of her shop and attempted to re-create it, there is no way I could ever totally replicate what she did, nor would I want to. In fact, most people don't really want to copy anyone. Most of us are just seeking inspiration, and seeing her store made me feel like mine was possible. I had no intention to steal her display ideas, I only wanted to keep a snapshot of that moment to keep me inspired to keep chasing my own dreams.

Ladies, hear me out: competition is dead. Modern, fearless female entrepreneurs know that there is enough room for everyone at the table. They are confident in their own abilities, and know that while we can technically do the same things, nobody can do them in the exact same way. They also see the power in connection. The energy that woman at that vintage pop-up spends "protecting" her store could be used generating new ideas, attracting abundance, and making meaningful bonds with other women.

Imagine if she would have let me take that photo? We probably would have started chatting, I definitely would have shared it on my Instagram, and who knows, maybe even some of my followers would have seen her store and went to check it out and shop with her. Perhaps our shared passion for vintage fashion could have even forged a future friendship. The entire experience would have energized the both of us, but instead, it drained us. I can't imagine she felt good treating me the way she did. And I certainly didn't feel good being treated like that.

It's time to break the old school rules and stop competing and start connecting. And we will get there by shifting our mindset. You have to tell yourself that there is enough success to go around for everyone, even if you aren't seeing sales yet, or bringing in your dream clients. Believing that the universe always provides is imperative to your success.

When you have a vision, and you work towards it consistently, and with a positive mentality, you'll start to notice that things begin to work out. Your outlook is everything, and when you remain in a space of optimism and possibility, the world looks totally different. Just like the woman in that vintage pop-up, you can choose to have a positive or a negative experience. You can choose to look at others as competition, or you can look at them as collaborators. And only one of those perspectives feels good.

You can choose your vibe. You can choose your energy. You can choose the space from which you operate from daily. Simply knowing that fact is powerful. I've met some of the most successful entrepreneurs on paper, meaning they have businesses that generate a ton of money, they're in positions most people would envy, and everything looks super glamorous, but they're miserable. They're constantly stressing out about what they don't have, or what could go wrong. They're living by the old rules: they're in a state of constant comparison and they're scared it could all go away. They're jealous of anyone who is a step ahead of them, and they certainly don't spend their time supporting others. They're choosing to live in a negative space, despite their success.

On the other hand, I've met some women who haven't even made a dollar in their business yet, but they're on cloud nine. They're flying high on their vision, and they're leaning into the unknown. They're excited about the future, and they're soaking in every part of their journey. They are choosing themselves, and choosing to live in a positive space, despite their circumstances. They're looking at other women as inspiration for what's possible. And *that* is what creates magic in your life and your business. This is the new paradigm of sisterhood. This is just the kind of next-level mindset we need to focus on to continue to challenge the status quo and create a new narrative for ourselves as women in business.

Hot Tips for Staying in Your Power

Audit your social media usage. Social media can be a great tool to keep us creatively inspired, but it can also make us feel like everyone is light years ahead of us and we're failing miserably. Whenever one of my clients or readers reaches out to me to tell me she's stuck, the first questions I usually ask her is, "How much time are you spending on

Instagram?" The answer is typically, "Too much." Please hear me with this one – tread lightly when it comes to who you follow online. Remind yourself that everyone is putting their best foot forward, and most people are not sharing their failures. Nobody is posting about the 749 things that went wrong in their business before that one incredible thing went right. Nobody is talking about the fear they must deal with daily as they continue to take risks. Nobody is talking about how isolating it can be to run a business, especially as a solo entrepreneur without a huge staff to discuss things with, or take on the tasks you don't feel like handling. Nobody is talking about the months where the money isn't coming in. Nobody is sharing how damn hard it is to make it all look like it's *not* hard.

If you find yourself feeling threatened, defeated, jealous, or stuck, I implore you to spend as much time offline as you possibly can. If you run your business primarily on social media, set a schedule for yourself. Bust out your planner, or your Google calendar, and schedule time to post, to respond to comments, or to check DMs. Schedule time to scroll your feed, as well. Perhaps you allow yourself 15 minutes a day to upload your posts, 1 hour a day to check comments and DMs, and 15 minutes a day to scroll. I guarantee that scheduling your social media time will be a significant reduction in the time you're mindlessly spending now.

I recently got the new iPhone and it has a tracker of how much time I spend on each of my apps. When I first checked out how much time I spend on social media, I was horrified. I run a huge part of my business through social media, and it's important to me to share and engage. But I've got to keep it all in check, and there has to be a point where I shut off. Just like any other job, we have to allow ourselves to disconnect. If not, we're sure to become overwhelmed and ultimately burn out. Most days, I try to hold off before checking my phone immediately when I wake up, and I try to stop checking it about an hour before bedtime so I can decompress. Going to sleep with images of stranger's days in my mind is not the way I want to wrap up my day, and I doubt it's the way you do, either. Use that precious time to express your gratitude for your own day, and set an intention for tomorrow.

Find your people. If you've fallen into the vibe of competition and you're living inside a space of lack, I urge you to make it a priority to find like-minded women. I cannot stress this enough, in fact, I've written about the importance of sisterhood in nearly all of my books. Finding a group of women, even if they don't live in your neighborhood and they're virtual friends at first, is crucial to your energy, and ultimately, your success. If you're hanging around women who constantly compare themselves to others, that's going to become your new normal. And it's a shitty place to be.

As I mentioned earlier, I spoke at a live event this year called *The Summit of Slay*, hosted by Jamie King, in Louisville, KY. I had no real expectations going into it, other than the fact that I came to serve the audience and would give it my best as always. Typically, when I speak at a conference, I do my thing and spend the rest of the time in my hotel room, working. But this event was *completely* different. The women who showed up were all there for one reason and one reason only – to connect. This went far beyond learning a few things from the women on stage. There was an energy of sisterhood that was palpable. So much so, that the other speakers and I wound up hanging out with the attendees the entire time. After our talks, when the day wrapped up, we all met up for drinks and talked for hours about business, life, love, and everything in between. We indulged in champagne-filled heart-to-hearts, where no topic was off-limits. We hung out well into the early morning hours. Nobody wanted to go back to their rooms!

A few of the attendees remarked that they were so surprised that the other speakers and I were so willing to spend time with them. How could we not? The vibe was undeniable and I wanted to soak it all in. That's the thing about energy – when it's there, it's hard to ignore. We all got something magical and unique from that weekend. We may have broken the typical "rules" or stepped out of the roles everyone plays at a conference of that nature, but who cares? We did what felt right. And it was epic.

Jump into your passion head first. When you create a safe space for other women to feel worthy, you inspire them to do the same for their communities. When you show the women around you that we're all equal, you push them to go further. During my session on stage, I made sure I stressed that message to the audience. The only difference between the women you see on stages, or read about in books, is that they just got started before you and stayed with it. That's it. The sooner you jump into the game, the sooner you find yourself on those stages and inside those books. Nobody is better than anyone else. We've all got a fair shot at this thing. Will you take yours?

Think about someone you secretly compete with in business. How does competing serve you?

____

____

What would it feel like to release the need to compete?

Who would you be if you built your business around sisterhood?

KEY TAKEAWAYS + NOTES

KEY TAKEAWAYS + NOTES

CHAPTER NINE

THERE IS ROOM FOR YOU AT THE TABLE

I recently woke up with a massive craving for avocado toast. Full disclosure: this happens often. But this morning in particular, the craving was impossible to ignore. With no avocados in sight, I knew my only hope would be an early morning run to the market to pick up my provisions; the most crucial being a beautiful, ripe avocado. I brushed my teeth, suited up into my leggings and faux fur coat, and headed to Trader Joe's.

I arrived promptly at 7:59 a.m., just moments before doors opened, tapping my feet, impatiently waiting to get in and grab the goods. While waiting, I noticed an independent fruit and vegetable stand on the sidewalk, directly across from the entrance to Trader Joe's. "He's got balls," I thought, as I surveyed this man's collection. It can't be easy to compete with a major retailer who sells the same things you do, at a lower cost, to boot.

The doors to Trader Joe's opened at 8:00 a.m. and I made a beeline to the avocado section, only to be instantly disappointed. Not only was the selection small, every avocado I touched was hard as a rock. I was shit out of luck. As I left the store, that independent fruit and vegetable stand caught my eye again. The owner smiled at me and said, "Good morning!" I walked over to check out *his* selection, and was pleasantly surprised to find an abundant mound of perfectly ripe avocados. I grabbed two and pulled out my wallet. "Have you seen these fresh raspberries?" he asked before taking my money. "And we have these amazing mangos too. They're delicious." Suddenly I found myself walking away with a bag of fresh fruit, totally impressed with this man's courage to fearlessly sell his fruit (which was actually much better) right next to his competition.

On my walk home, I started thinking about business. I can't even begin to tell you how many women I've coached who have all come to me with the same concern. They feel like their industries are saturated, everything has been done before, and it's pointless to even bother showing up. They get in their own heads so deeply that all of their creativity is completely zapped. They sabotage their dreams before they ever let them become a reality. They talk themselves out of their ideas before they ever have a chance to bloom because they assume there is no room left for them at the table. And that's just untrue.

Believe me when I tell you this: we need you. We need everything you have to offer. And we need it in the way that only *you* can provide it.

A few weeks ago, I put out a call looking for a virtual assistant to help me with a project. I received dozens of emails and applications from women who all essentially do the same thing. However, a handful of those women really stood out to me. It wasn't because they had more experience, or even came with glowing referrals. It was the style in which they reached out. It was their own personal flair that attracted me to them. It was their energy.

And here's the thing – the people I'm most authentically connected to may not be the people you're most authentically connected to. That's the beauty of being real and raw and *you*.

My friend Noa, who I've talked your ear off about in this book, does these sing-alongs every so often in our SoulCycle class. He'll pick a fun song, like *Tiny Dancer* by Elton John, and ask the whole room to sing the chorus. If everyone is brave enough to belt out the lyrics, you'll hear about 66 people singing, and it sounds amazing. But in most cases, only a couple of people are bold enough to sing at first. And it sounds like crap. With some further priming from Noa, a few more voices trickle in by the second chorus. And then by the third (can you tell I've been through this a few times?), Noa has convinced everyone to sing, and we sound like a full-fledged choir. Okay, fine, maybe more like a bar of happy drunk people. But we sound good! And most importantly, it's a blast.

So how does Noa get everyone to eventually chime in? He reminds us that our voices are not just important – they are necessary. And a few voices don't hold the same power as all of our voices working together. Everyone is needed. Even the person who is leaning on the rider next to them to do the work and sing louder. It's safe to say this is a powerful metaphor for what needs to happen in this world right now, don't you think?

If you struggle with feeling like your voice doesn't matter, or you don't have anything exciting to offer this world, here are some tips to pull you out of that mindset and get you into that delicious place of ingenuity and creativity we all love to be in.

Take a digital detox. Take a few hours off. Take a few days off if you're ballsy enough (I highly recommend this if you can). Pull yourself away from the internet and get out and live! The experiences you have offline will energize you and get you back to where you need to be in no time. You'll also realize there's a big, beautiful world out there beyond Instagram.

Create a personal power mantra. Writing and repeating a mantra that reminds you of your power is key. Something like, "I have been given a vision for a reason, and I am worthy of bringing beautiful things to this world. People love what I have to offer." Repeat this mantra each morning when you wake up, and whenever you're about to start working on that thing you love.

Get real with yourself. It's easy to look around on social media and think everyone is 10 steps ahead of you and get swept up in a pity party, but the reality is everyone started somewhere. Remind yourself that all of the big ideas that inspire you were all seeds of thought at one time. The playing field is even in the universe. It's up to you to bust through all the negative thoughts and keep showing up to see your vision through. Remember, there are people out there with less talent and experience than you who are killing it. The only difference? They started sooner and stuck with it.

So please know that you matter. There is room for you at the table. Let go of the fear, put your blinders on, and get to work. We're waiting for you.

KEY TAKEAWAYS + NOTES

KEY TAKEAWAYS + NOTES

PART THREE:

BLAZE YOUR OWN TRAIL

CHAPTER TEN

IT'S NEVER TOO LATE TO BE WHO YOU SECRETLY DREAM OF BEING

Phil Wohl once said, "Reinvention is the purest form of hope" and I've never resonated with a quote more. I have reinvented my mindset, my business, my perspective, my personal style, my habits, my thoughts, my values, and my actions so many times. And I'm still doing it. And every single time there is a deep, underlying feeling of hope sparking that change. A desire to do more, be more, and fulfill my greatest potential as a human being.

My only rule? It's never too late.

A few years ago, I decided to dye my hair pink. I was thirty-six years old. My decision went beyond the fact that I loved pink hair; it was an opportunity for me to express myself in a way that I never had before. It was a chance to step into a bolder, more badass version of myself. Having pink hair was a powerful experience that allowed me to face my fears and be "seen" in a new way. There was no more blending in with a cotton-candy-colored head! My hair was a conversation starter, and I found myself chatting up more strangers than ever before. And most of them were looking for permission to do something bold in their lives, too.

For me, dying my hair pink represented independence and rebellion. It represented breaking away from the corporate chains I felt tied to for so many years, and embracing my role in the world as a rule-breaking, do-it-my-way kind of woman. It felt liberating and exciting and it inspired me creatively.

Before I dyed my hair, I struggled with that nagging, "Who does she think she is?" voice in my head more times than I can count. I wondered if people would think I was having some kind of early mid-life crisis or breakdown. I wondered if people would still take me seriously as a professional. I had to push those fears aside and channel my most courageous self to actually go for it. I had to be inspired by the women I admire and ask myself what *they* would do? I had to stop racking up a Pinterest board full of inspirational photos and become my own permission slip. And once I did, I unlocked a sense of self-confidence that I never knew I could feel.

I went from "I wish I could pull that off" to *I am pulling that off.* That's a bold transition and empowering place to be.

While we're on the topic of pink hair, I want to formally introduce you to my former client and friend, Jamie King, aka "The Slay Coach." I mentioned Jamie briefly earlier in the book, but it's time you get to know her a bit better. There's a lot you can learn from this purple-haired passionista, especially when it comes to pivoting into something new and reinventing yourself.

Jamie got into entrepreneurship after leaving her corporate sales career in search of freedom. She fell into network marketing, working with a predominant health and fitness company, but never felt completely at home in that industry. Though she admittedly drank her shakes and "worked out-ish", she realized she was more passionate about the business-building side of the job. Jamie's passion was not found in the products, as it typically should be in network marketing, but more in the mentoring aspect of helping women create their own empires.

I had Jamie on my podcast, *Style Your Mind*, a few months ago and we had a real and raw conversation about what it looks like to make a sharp and clear pivot in your career and have fun while doing it. You can, and should, listen to the full interview, but I want to share some highlights with you in this chapter as it relates to self-reinvention, because there's a lot you can learn from this powerhouse.

When I asked Jamie about what it was like to leave her network marketing role and step out on her own as a business coach, she told me that her physical rebrand was just as important as her business re-brand. Not only did she totally shift gears in her career, she embraced a whole new persona. "I did a very distinct rebrand when I pivoted from health and fitness coaching to then business mentoring. And for me that was purple hair, that was new branding, a new logo. I kind of created my alter ego," she explained. "I was a huge Jem and the Holograms fan when I was a kid and I always wanted to be Jem. I wanted to have the bright purple hair, I wanted to wear the sequins and glitter and if ya'll see my closet…I'm wearing pink and purple right now. I've always wanted to do that. So I thought, what would I do at age five or ten? How would I dress? How would I act? Would I be playful? Would I be afraid to talk to people? No. Would I be afraid to tell everyone what I was doing or what I was passionate about? No! So who is that real, authentic self? I think your branding comes from who we always saw ourselves as-as a kid."

Jamie admits being nervous to make the shift. She was afraid of what people would think about her, but she moved forward anyway. She hired a coach who helped her not only develop her new business, but the mindset required to pivot with confidence and create a new world for herself.

She also tapped into the confidence she had in her corporate career. Even though she eventually moved on, she realized in retrospect that she had been branding herself all along – even when she was in Corporate America. We chatted about her ideas on branding and how to stand out without selling out, whether you're an entrepreneur or you're working a traditional job.

"I've been able to move up corporate ladders very quickly, with no education. I have no college degree. I should not have been making the money that I was making in Corporate America. I should not have had the position that I had. And I remember people saying to me at that level of 'success' or whatever, I got this great promotion to Site Leader, I managed a call center. I was travelling 15-20 weeks out of the year, going on all these fancy trips, first class, all the fun things and expense accounts, credit cards, phones, like it was just the corporate life. I was 24, and the youngest one of my peers that was the closest in age to me was like 10 years older than me, like 34, 35. And so I was looked at by my peers and I even heard comments that had been said about me, like 'Oh, well, who did she sleep with to get to this position? Oh, well, she's young and she's pretty, that's why she got her job.'

What got me that job was asking for it, was building a brand based on being this young, fun, hard-working, funny girl who wears makeup and dresses pretty. I always dressed fun and different, and people would be like 'What are you wearing?' I didn't realize at the time that was branding, but I had this thing where I was the chick that loved to drink bourbon and go out with the guys and watched football but I also loved makeup and I also was funny and I also like just talk to everyone. I made friends with everyone."

Jamie admits that when she moved into network marketing, she struggled. "For years, when I was trying to build a business online, I wasn't getting any traction because I was literally just copying and pasting what other people were doing." Once she gave herself permission to be herself again, to passionately chase what she truly wanted, and to burn the rule book of who she should be, she thrived.

I think it's also important to point out the fact that Jamie was in her thirties when she rebranded. A lot of women are terrified that it's "too late" to make a shift – especially when it comes to their personal style – and that's just untrue. They're living by some imaginary rule book where they think they're not allowed to have fun past a certain point in life. It breaks my heart to see women using age as a reason for not going after their dreams. I understand where the mindset comes from; we live in a world where most people are just focused on the status quo. They go to college, get a decent job, get married, buy a house, have a kid or two, retire, and die. I hate to sound so morbid, but isn't that the path most people you know are on?

It's time to challenge the status quo. It's time to raise a middle finger to the timelines and group thinking that make us feel like we're meant to be on some bullshit path that ultimately leads to nowhere.

I collected a few examples of self-made women who are considered "late bloomers" according to the rules of society. In my opinion, they're right on time. Let's take a moment to honor these incredible women and make a mental note of when they achieved their greatest success.

Anna Wintour. I call her "Auntie Anna" and she is for sure one of my secret mentors. She's full of powerful wisdom and savvy advice that applies to all women in business. We all know her as the sunglass-clad editor-in-chief of *Vogue* magazine, but she didn't actually land that job until she was 39 years old. Anna previously worked at magazines, but not always the kind of magazines you might think. She held the role of fashion editor at *Viva* – an erotic women's magazine – for years before she arrived at *Vogue.* Our takeaway here is that you've got to start somewhere, and you can't be ashamed of where that "somewhere" is. And Anna proves to us that when you stay the course and commit to your craft, you can become iconic.

Julia Child. Would you believe she didn't even learn to cook until she was 36 years old? Julia had big dreams to be a writer, and even submitted her plays and short stories to *The New Yorker*, which were never published. She followed her passion for food and learned to cook, and landed her first TV show at age 50, which was eventually syndicated to 96 stations. She went on to publish the best-selling cookbook *Mastering the Art of French Cuisine* and her name is now synonymous with cooking. Our takeaway here is that your curiosities may lead you to your biggest successes.

Toni Morrison. We know her as one of the greatest authors of all time, but Toni Morrison was actually working behind the scenes for the first half of her career. In the 1960s, Toni worked as an editor at Random House while raising her two sons as a single mother. Her novel, *The Bluest Eye*, wasn't published until she was 39 years old. Although it was well-received by critics, it actually did not sell well. Her next novel, *Sula*, was nominated for an American Book Award, which she didn't win. But then came her third novel, *Song of Solomon*, and that's where things really took off. That book won the National Books Critic award and really put Toni on the map. She was 46 years old. She went on to receive a Pulitzer and Nobel prize for literature.

These women should serve as an example that it is never too late to be who you secretly dream of being. You can change your mind. At any time. For any reason. You don't need permission. And you certainly don't owe anyone an explanation.

Boldly choose to change, transform, and ascend into your higher self. Boldly choose be the woman you want to be. Every time a woman unapologetically evolves, she creates space for other women to do the same. Every time a woman chooses herself, she shows other women it's okay to choose *themselves*, too.

A few questions for you to think about:

What would my life look like if I boldly stepped into the best version of myself?

What would it feel like if I could allow myself to evolve without apology?

What would I be doing right now if I burned the rule book and did what I truly wanted to do?

I encourage you stay open to reinventing yourself. To stay wide-eyed and interested in life. To be fully alive is the greatest gift in the world. I know life can become demanding, overwhelming, and sometimes downright depressing. But we've got to remember that we have the power to shift, in any moment we choose.

So chase every single curiosity and follow every single obsession. You never know where they will lead you. If you're lucky, they'll bring you closer to a life filled with hope. Don't allow yourself to become seduced by mediocrity. Believe that there is more for you – because there is.

KEY TAKEAWAYS + NOTES

KEY TAKEAWAYS + NOTES

CHAPTER ELEVEN

THE BEAUTY IN BEING A BEST-CASE SCENARIO GIRL

It's a Friday afternoon in April and I'm on the phone with one of my coaching clients, who happens to be a very accomplished nurse practitioner who runs her own wellness center. We'll call her Jen, to protect her privacy. Jen is stressed to the max about the hours she's putting in, which are now six full days a week seeing clients and handling all the medical billing and admin work. Like many of us, it's difficult for her to delegate, so she just does it all herself. She wants to do even more, because she truly loves her job, but she is about to break.

As her coach, I know we need a creative solution.

"What about closing the office on Fridays so you can get a real day off?" I ask. She immediately shuts me down. "There is no WAY I can do that! What if somebody needs me? What if I wind up losing patients?" I allow her to run through every worst-case scenario she can possibly think of.

"What if none of that happens? What if this is winds up being the best thing you ever do for your business – and yourself?"

She pauses.

"I guess I can give it a try in July after I travel."

Jen winds up closing her office for 2 Fridays in July. It winds up being the best thing she ever did for her business, and herself. She feels freer and less anxious almost immediately. She implements a new rule about being closed every Friday, and she is now traveling regularly to her weekend home, studying for her doctorate degree, getting massages, and going shopping. All because she decided to give herself permission to imagine the best-case scenario.

I want you to think about a time in your life where you were focused on the worst-case scenario. Maybe you were waiting on some news that you were so sure would be bad, so you spent days, if not weeks, obsessing over what could possibly go wrong. Maybe you were launching your business and you found yourself completely entrenched in negative thoughts, wondering if and when you were going to fail.

Now, I want you to think about what actually happened. I can bet that most likely, it didn't turn out as badly as you thought it would. In fact, I might even venture to guess it turned out pretty damn well. But what about all that time you spent stressing yourself out? What about all that precious energy you poured into worrying about absolutely nothing? What else could you have done with that time that you'll never get back? It's kind of a sobering thought, right?

There is one major habit that prevents women from being happy and successful, and living a generally good life, and that is being a Worst-Case Scenario Girl. Have you ever been in a situation where you really want something to happen, or you're working really hard at something in your business, or your life, and your mind automatically starts going to the "What if this doesn't work out?" zone? I think we've all been there. Questions like, "What if I can't get approved for this mortgage?" or "What if the clients don't come?" or "What if it all falls apart?" pop up and take over our minds like a cancer.

I've had a lot of clients and friends fall into this category (and I have too, to be totally honest) and here's what I always ask them. What if it doesn't work out? What is the actual worst thing that can happen? Once we identify that, then we can realize it's not as scary as we think. Because at the end of the day, you'll deal with it. You will either find another way to make it happen, or you will survive if it doesn't. You will move on. You will be okay. You've survived 100% of your bad days, and you're still here. There's power in knowing that.

My next response is, what if it *does* work out? What if you get every single thing you want? What if you got your hopes up? Would that be so bad? There are so many benefits of being a Best-Case Scenario Girl. Being optimistic and imagining things actually working out for you is incredibly important in nurturing your mental health, your physical health, your business, and ultimately feeling successful.

And this isn't just some random thought, either. There's science to back this up. Dr. John Medina, affiliate professor of bioengineering at the University of Washington School of Medicine and author of *Brain Rules*, actually says that optimism can increase your life span by nearly eight years. It can also help ward off depression, by aiding the brain in releasing the neurotransmitter dopamine. According to a Forbes article where Dr. Medina was interviewed, "Optimism not only reduces stress, but it also promotes the production of the neurotransmitter dopamine. 'Dopamine packs a serious wallop,' Medina says. He likens dopamine to the ignition system in your car. 'Insert the key into the lock, and the car springs to life.' Dopamine begins to fade as we age—beginning in our thirties. But we don't want dopamine to decline. Dopamine makes us happy, increases motivation, and is even responsible for giving entrepreneurs the courage to take risks. As Medina says, 'Dopamine is a big deal.'"

When I was first beginning to think about leaving my corporate job at MTV around 2013 to pursue my new vision for my life, I was doing all the math, planning all the details, and doing a wonderful job at imagining it all going to shit. I'd sit there and ask myself things like, what if I can't pay my bills? What if I have to move back in with my mom? What if I can't afford health insurance? What if I can't drink my favorite champagne? What if this just doesn't work? All legitimate questions, but also questions that did absolutely nothing to help move me forward.

And you know what happened at the end of 2013? I didn't leave MTV. I stayed in that situation for another long year, frazzled and filled with anxiety and depression, knowing I deserved more, but paralyzed by my own fear. I still felt like somewhere, deep down, I needed permission to quit. I wasn't ready to break the rules I had created for myself inside some desperate quest to "do the right thing." I needed everyone to back me up and tell me I was doing the right thing by leaving. I needed everyone on board because I couldn't figure out a way to completely get on board myself. If they all gave me permission, then maybe, just maybe, it wouldn't be so scary.

Things started to shift in 2014. I decided the old way wasn't working, and I needed a new mindset. Burnt out from obsessing over my fears, I started to imagine the best-case scenario. I started to visualize my success. I became optimistic about the future – excited, even. I started to picture myself walking into my boss' office and handing over my resignation letter with confidence and certainty. I stared to imagine days where I felt fired up, fulfilled, and creative. And I just simply decided to shut out all the noise that kept me stuck.

Before we go on, I do want to clear something up. Being a Best-Case Scenario Girl does not mean you don't have to put in the work. I've seen a trend lately where there seems to be this glamorization of manifestation. Where people are convinced that if they just think about something enough, it will happen. I hear people talking about how they manifested a seven-figure business or a beach house or a trip to Bali and they fail to mention all of the steps they actually took to bring those things to fruition. There is a serious problem with this messaging. There is an enormous amount of hard work, repetitive inspired action, and grind that goes into creating your ideal life. It's a gentle balance between faith, and hard-ass work.

When you're imagining the best-case scenario, you're freeing up the space in your mind and your energy so you can get out there and do that work. You're removing the mental clutter and those negative fantasies. And by removing all that clutter, you're giving yourself space to get creative and strategic. You're elevating your dopamine levels and you're feeling happier. When I started to imagine the best-case scenario for myself in 2014, I started to move.

Fueled by optimistic thoughts, I got strategic about my time. I used my paid time off (sick days and vacation days) to build my business. Essentially, I set myself up so MTV paid me to create an escape plan. I decided to view my full-time job as my angel investor. That money coming in was no longer suffocating me with the thoughts of permanence and fear; instead, it was a temporary gift that I could use to create my best-case scenario. And that is exactly what I did.

By the end of 2014, I walked away from MTV and never looked back. I know that the only way I was able to pull that off was by ditching the fear and investing in my faith. I chose to look ahead with confidence and clarity and not muddy up my thinking with all the scary "what-ifs." And that's what has made all the difference.

Since 2014, I've more than tripled my six-figure corporate salary, earned over half a million dollars self-publishing my own books, built a booming, worldwide coaching practice, created a podcast that now has over six million listeners and growing, been featured in media outlets like Forbes, Success, Entrepreneur, Marie Claire, Cosmo, and more – and that's just a few of the highlights of my career so far.

Imagine I had just kept focusing on what could go wrong?

I want you to think about a situation where you find yourself thinking negatively. Where are you defaulting to the worst-case scenario?

____

____

____

____

____

How would it feel to release that mindset and imagine only the best things happening for you?

____

____

____

____

____

Write your best-case scenario fantasy:

KEY TAKEAWAYS + NOTES

KEY TAKEAWAYS + NOTES

CHAPTER TWELVE

WHAT ARE YOU AVAILABLE FOR?

As we grow into the next-level version of ourselves, it's important to regularly check in on our energy. With more success, comes more demands. We're required to make more decisions, engage with more people, and the stakes get higher. There's often more money on the table, more risks involved, and a bigger platform to serve and share from.

And it's a lot.

As I become more successful in my own life, I've had to think a lot about what I do with my time, and who I let into my world, and who I let have access to me. I once saw a quote that really struck me. I'm paraphrasing here, but it was along the lines of this: "This chapter of my life requires me to be a little bit less accessible. This chapter of my life requires me to be a little bit more private."

I know whenever I feel overwhelmed with work, I get this feeling of wanting to shut off to the world at certain points in the day, whether it's at night or in the morning, and protect my energy. I give so much of myself, whether it's through the podcast or through my social media or my Instagram stories or my books or my blog. My job is to give. And I truly love what I do and feel so fortunate that people actually want me to give to them. But I'm also a recovering people pleaser, so the *way* I give is something I need to be mindful of.

People pleasing is not just about wanting to see people be happy, because I think most of us do want that; it's wanting to see people happy at the expense of your own happiness. It's giving people things to satisfy them and in turn giving things up in your *own* life. Not a good habit.

It's scary sometimes to say "no" to people. It's scary sometimes to think that we may be letting someone down, but what's even scarier is thinking about living the rest of your life for someone else. Think about that - it's scarier to live the rest of your life prioritizing everyone's happiness over your own, rather than potentially letting someone down in the moment. And something that I've come to understand when it comes to boundary setting, is that most of the time people *do* understand when you have to say no.

When it comes to privacy and boundaries and creating new standards for your life, you must know that that nobody else's sense of peace and nobody else's sense of happiness is more important than your own. You must ask yourself, on a daily basis, "What am I available for?" Are you available for frantic energy, exhaustion, and overserving those around you? Or are you available for peace, privacy, and control over your time and energy?

I have officially become the person who doesn't always see or respond to all of my social media comments. I have officially become the person that doesn't always answer text messages. I have officially become the person who says "no" - a lot, who turns her phone off for hours at a time, who no longer feels guilty for the people I can't get to, who no longer feels guilty for cancelling on people or events, and I'm not sorry.

Of course, I do it all with kindness and respect. And I do keep my word when it comes to meaningful commitments or business arrangements. I'd never blow something major off unless it was a true emergency. But there are times I just need a break, and I know that canceling a dinner with friends is the right choice in that moment. Or responding to a text message the following day is totally okay.

I remember years ago, thinking I will never be *that person.* I judged those who weren't on top of every single thing in their lives. I prided myself on being able to be everything to everyone. All the time. I was so damn naïve. Being unavailable does not mean we're not working hard or not caring for others. In fact, I think it's the opposite. Being unavailable means I'm choosing me. It means I'm nurturing my own mind, body and soul so that I can continue to give, expand and evolve. We cannot pour from an empty cup. We can't even pour from a half-full cup. I have learned that my cup needs to be overflowing before I can even think about being there for anyone else.

Every new level of success requires we create a new set of boundaries to protect our spirit. To those who are on the rise and struggling with overwhelm, please know that you cannot and should not do it all. The number of women I see, myself included, breaking under this insurmountable stress is alarming. Take time. Breathe. Say no. Turn the phone off. Write a new rule book for your life. Redefine what success looks like for you and make sure your happiness and your peace are the first things on that damn list.

When the news broke that Kate Spade had committed suicide in 2018, it hit me hard. Suicide is tragic. Sadly, I've heard of far too many untimely deaths from suicide, but many were difficult for me to relate to, until Kate. Kate Spade was a well-respected business woman who created an incredible brand all about celebrating women. The

Kate Spade brand was about joy and sparkle and bliss. So how could this happen? How could a woman who created a business so supercharged with happiness take her own life? It took my breath away.

After Kate's death, I started a conversation with my readers about mental health and the importance of talking about it openly. About being okay with saying, "Hey, I think I need to talk to someone," or "I just need to know I'm not alone." I think sometimes we can look at women on the outside who are ultra-successful, beautiful, wealthy, and in a position of power, and we assume that everything is perfect. We assume that their lives are glossy and beautiful and pretty and Instagrammable and that there are never any problems. But we never take a step back to realize that everyone is fighting a battle that we know nothing about.

I'm sure many people had no idea that Kate was fighting her own demons, and I am sure there are women in your own life right now that you know that are struggling with something. Maybe it's anxiety or maybe it's depression or maybe it's feeling like they're not good enough. It's something to think about. Check in with them, especially the strong ones, and ask them if they're okay. Check in with yourself. *Are you okay?*

I recently returned home from a whirlwind weekend of work events in Miami. The events were incredible, but business travel always takes a toll on me. As much as I love connecting with my readers, I also recognize that I am pouring into people non-stop. And if I don't immediately take time to pour back into myself, I'm in trouble. As soon as I landed, I hit the ground running again in New York City. Clients, calls, emails— I was overwhelmed to say the least. I felt myself reaching the breaking point, in tears, wondering how I was going to get through the day and get it all done. I desperately prayed for a few minutes of solitude so I could catch my breath. And then I heard about Kate Spade. And I finally understood why someone would just want out. No matter how stressful things get, I would never, ever, in a million years, consider taking my own life. I love my life. I know that it is precious and I feel so fortunate to be in this place. However, I can understand how things can get out of control and how you can suddenly find yourself just buried and just gasping for air and trying to find a way to get through the day.

Someone once told me, "With every level, comes a new devil." With every rise on the road to success, every time you level up, there are more people who want to bring you down. There are more challenges, there are more things to do in a day, there are more expectations on you. It's time we start having more compassion for the women around us. It's time we start having more compassion for ourselves.

I used to get really offended if someone didn't get back to me right away. If someone didn't text me back, or someone didn't email me back, I took it personally and felt rejected. And now that I'm in the position I am in, I realize we can't be everything to everyone. Sometimes, I can't answer a text message. Sometimes, I can't go to someone's event and now I understand it's okay.

I hope this perspective helps you think about your own boundaries and who and what you're allowing into your energetic space. Please remember that your mental health is your number one priority. There is nothing in this world, in your career, in a relationship, in a business partnership, that is worth your peace of mind. You are never alone. If you need to reach out for help, please do. Please do not hesitate to get what you need. There is always a sunrise after the darkest of nights.

In the space below, write about the new boundaries you need to create for yourself:

____

____

____

____

____

KEY TAKEAWAYS + NOTES

KEY TAKEAWAYS + NOTES

CHAPTER THIRTEEN

YOU CAN'T BE A VICTIM AND A SUCCESS AT THE SAME TIME

I don't make a habit of this, but I'll occasionally read the 1-star reviews of my books, and other books in the personal development space on Amazon. While I know what others think about me (and others) is none of my business, I like to check and see if there is a common thread of critique when it comes to the messaging women leaders are putting out there. And sometimes, I'll be able to glean some constructive feedback from those reviews, but for the most part, the bad reviews are littered with ignorant and judgmental comments from other women bashing me – and my fellow authors – for our success.

"She referenced SoulCycle!" Or "She had a nanny helping with her kids!" Or my personal favorite, "She just got lucky."

It happens all over social media, too. I follow a fashion entrepreneur that I adore. She's humble, stylish, and so generous with her content. She recently had a baby, and she is honest about the help she has been able to receive. She works hard, and decided to hire a night nurse so that she could sleep the first few months while her new baby adjusted to his sleep schedule. She shared a rude and judgmental comment she received from one of her Instagram followers who called her "unrelatable" because of her choice to have help and said she had to unfollow her.

What on earth does this woman's night nurse have to do with her content? And why would another woman make her feel badly for getting the help that she desires to take care of her child? I was floored by this, but sadly, it's all too common. Women are still shaming other women for their success. And it's bullshit.

I will admit that I've caught myself dimming my own light because I was worried about making someone else feel badly. I've silenced myself on more than one occasion because I didn't want to come across as "bragging" about something I was extremely proud of. But all that does is keep *all* women small. All that does is perpetuate a cycle of women feeling ashamed of their success. Every time a woman rises up and celebrates herself, she shows another woman that it's okay to do the same. Every time a woman showcases her wins, she shows another woman that it's possible to achieve great things. When you choose that perspective, you owe it to the world to shout about your success from the rooftops!

We must celebrate women *without* condition. We must realize that we all come from different walks of life, backgrounds, and sets of opportunity. Some are more fortunate than others, that's just a fact. Some will have every single door opened for them and a red carpet rolled out to boot. But I've learned that spending my energy being mad at those women does nothing to bolster my own success. Trying to figure out who had it easier is a losing game. It drains the hell out of me and makes me feel like shit. Remember: we're all responsible for our own lives. We've all got to work the hand we're dealt. We can't be a victim and a success at the same time – so choose your stance.

I was raised by a single mother. My father sold drugs my entire life, then did them, so much so to the point that my mom had no choice but to leave him and raise us alone because he snorted away every penny we had. Sometimes, she'd carry a light bulb from room to room because she couldn't afford to get another one until her next paycheck. We grew up broke, but I never let that stand in my way from designing a life where I wouldn't be broke as an adult. And I certainly never let my past define me.

I have worked for every single thing I have. I had zero connections, but I had a drive like no other because I knew that I had to make things happen for myself. I took odd jobs from the age of fifteen, even sweeping up a makeup shop in exchange for classes because my mom couldn't afford to pay for them for me and I really wanted to learn how to do makeup. I bent over backwards at every internship I had, coming in early, staying late, and doing the jobs nobody else wanted to do. I built sold relationships with others and leveraged every single opportunity in front of me. I went *all in* on my future.

Nobody got me in the door at my job at MTV - I did. I applied to dozens of jobs there, and when I was finally offered a position, even though it certainly wasn't my dream job, I jumped on it and treated it like gold. I worked my ass off, working from 8 a.m. - 11 p.m. many nights, sometimes even setting my alarm in the middle of the night to wake up and check on ad campaigns. My boss got fired shortly after I was hired, and I stepped up and filled in the role, with no management experience, at the age of twenty-six. I built an entire team, negotiated multiple promotions for myself, and took that job and turned it into a career.

Eventually, I decided I wasn't happy at MTV, and it wasn't going to be a long-term deal for me. But I couldn't just quit. I had bills to pay, and health insurance to provide. In fact, when I was serious about leaving MTV, I really had no choice but to stay at least another year because my husband had been laid off from his job and I had to support the both of us. I couldn't walk away, but I could make positive changes. I could take *action*. I enrolled in life coaching school, took classes at night three times a week, and became a certified professional life coach. I hustled at night and on weekends to get clients while still doing a stellar job as a director at MTV with a team of now twenty people under me. I wrote three books from my cubicle. I built a blog. I did so much more that I can't even write here because this would become a novel.

I finally set myself up with enough side hustle income and enough faith in myself to know I could make it work. I quit MTV after eight years and went full-time in my business. I talk about my "story" a lot. In my books. On my podcast. As often as I can without letting my past define me and become my entire story. But then I read those crappy, presumptuous Amazon reviews or see nasty social media comments and I feel so sad. Not because I feel I need to explain myself to anyone, but because people make assumptions about others all the time. They assume women who have something couldn't possibly have earned it themselves. They assume women who love their lives aren't "real."

Or they blame the woman who did have a leg up, or did start out with more money or opportunity. They blame her for their own lack of success, like somehow, she is responsible for that. I'll say it again: we need to celebrate each other *without condition*. We need to realize that every woman is real, regardless of her background, her bank account, her story, or her love for Chanel. We need to not feel guilty for having a booming business, beautiful shoes, hired help, or whatever else makes us sparkle. We deserve it all.

And most importantly, we need to realize that we rise by lifting others, not by trying to drag them down.

KEY TAKEAWAYS + NOTES

KEY TAKEAWAYS + NOTES

CHAPTER FOURTEEN

WHY NOT YOU?

In 2018, I began receiving messages from more and more Iranian woman who were finding my book, Girl Code, in their local libraries in Iran. One of these women in particular thanked me and shared with me that it gave her hope of pursuing her dreams despite the challenges she, and the women of her county face.

At the time of writing this book, women in Iran constitute 19% of the workforce and that number has only increased 7% since 1990. To offer any kind of hope and inspire any kind of change to those women through my words is an absolute privilege and honor.

I was in no special position when I wrote *Girl Code*; in fact, I was in quite a risky one. I'm a regular girl from Brooklyn who dropped out of college to go work. I had a vision for my life and I couldn't wait to get there, and the things they were teaching me in school just weren't working for me. Raised by a single mother who did an incredible job even though we were dead broke, I am a first-generation entrepreneur with no fancy mentors or leg up other than a hardcore belief in my-self. I didn't have rich parents with connections, so hustling quickly became my second language and I took job after job, all in an effort to keep learning, growing, and connecting with others. As I explained in the previous chapter, my success was always up to me, and I now know that was the biggest blessing of all.

In 2014, I walked out of Corporate America with $7,000 in my bank account (my entire life savings, which came from a performance bonus I received at work the day before I resigned) and took a chance on myself. I wrote and self-published *Girl Code* from my kitchen table in my little Brooklyn apartment and somehow it took on a life of its own. It has now crossed oceans and transcended cultures. It's been translated into seven languages, and according to many of my readers, saved their lives. That right there goes to show you the power of an idea in motion.

We all have this ability. You never know who may stumble upon your words someday, but first, you must put them out there. You must ask yourself, "why not me?" Why can't you be the change agent?

Around 2014, I met a woman named Noelle Santos on the internet. Neither of us can recall exactly how we "met," but we both recall Noelle contacting me through Snapchat, asking for advice around an idea she had to bring a bookstore to the Bronx, where none existed at the time. At the time, Noelle was working a cushy, corporate job on Wall Street, earning six-figures and putting her accounting degree to good use. She was comfortable, but after seeing a petition on Facebook to urge her local congress members to build a bookstore in the Bronx after the last Barnes & Noble went out of business, she became extremely *uncomfortable*.

The Bronx is a borough of 1.5 million people and ten colleges, and also Noelle's hometown, where she currently lives. Furious and frustrated, she signed the petition, but immediately decided she wasn't about to wait for the politics to align to get her bookstore. And in that moment, she got to work.

I sat down with Noelle recently at The Lit Bar, the bookstore/wine bar she built herself from the ground-up five years later after crowdfunding support and a whole lot of hustle. As we sipped on our wine (she had a Cab, I had a Chardonnay), we reminisced on those earlier conversations we had as she was rallying to get the store created. We talked about the importance of choosing yourself to get things done. We talked about the criticism she's faced despite her good intentions, and the daily challenges that arise while embarking on a brand-new industry. To hear our whole conversation, make sure you listen to the full episode on my podcast, *Style Your Mind.*

I asked Noelle the first thing she did after deciding she was going to build this bookstore. "I Googled 'How to open a bookstore," she told me. A tip she says she learned after one of my rants online. Ha!

"The first thing that came up was The American Booksellers Association, which is our Trade Association for the industry. They had a checklist called *Owning a Bookstore.* First thing to do was to attend this class in Amelia Island, Florida, never heard of it. So I took a week off work and went."

Noelle wound up meeting someone in the class who had previously entered a business plan competition through Citibank. He didn't win, but he thought Noelle would do great, so he encouraged her to enter. She entered, with no expectations other than getting some resources she could use for her mission, and she won. "I beat 358 startups in New York City, with the exception of Queens because they have their own competition. I won $8,000 from that and then I used that money to launch a pop-up shop because I wanted to test the market, to see if this was actually viable. It was in my heart at this moment, but you know, I didn't know if it was actually going to be a sustainable business. So, I assessed the market. I started by starting a book club on www.meetup.com. Now we're the biggest book club in New York City and we actually meet in person."

Aside from the pop up and book club, Noelle found other ways to learn the industry so she could prepare herself for opening the store. She decided to start interning after work at bookstores and cafes so she could get hands-on experience and connect with people in the industry she wanted to be in. "I humbled myself. I would take off my suit and walk to Housing Works and bake cookies and carry boxes of wine and shelve at Greenlight bookstore in Brooklyn and learn the register at Word Up Community Bookshop in exchange for mentorship. I'm like 'What can I do for you, for free? Can I ask you questions while I'm working?'" she told me. "I worked for free on nights and weekends and then I continued to go down the checklist."

Now that The Lit Bar is up and running (and has become very successful, I should add), Noelle's job has just begun. She faces her fears daily and has to continue to adapt to an ever-changing industry, but she wouldn't have it any other way. She also says that creating this business has restored her faith in humanity. When I asked her how she has been able to find such incredible support, she says, "By just being me. I represent a very specific demographic. I'm from the South Bronx. I was born and raised in Soundview, lived in this area for my entire life, went to college here and I am very much a product of my environment. I grew up with the whole stereotypical South Bronx upbringing, you know with my family and all of that and hip hop is very much a part of me, my lingo, who I am, and I show up that way. No one's representing us in the publishing industry, in the book industry, not at the scale or with the investment that I would like to see it done at. So, me being myself was like filing a void in the market and people gravitated towards that."

Noelle is a beautiful example of choosing yourself and creating whatever you wish to see in the world. Nothing was handed to her; she had to make it happen for herself and her community, and she did it. And she continues to do it every single day. She is a leader and a lighthouse and an ongoing inspiration for me. And I hope that by learning about her story, she can be for you, too.

I'm sure at this point, you're thinking about *that thing*. That thing you so desperately want to build or create but for some reason, you've held off. For some reason, you've told yourself that you can't, or that the timing isn't right, or that you're not the one to do it.

Let's get to the root of that. Let's get to the root of why perhaps you haven't felt like *you* could be the one who makes an impact in this world. What has been holding you back? What are you afraid of? For many, it's the fear of what others will think. *Who does she think she is? Who is she to write that book? Who is she to grow that multi-million-dollar business? Who is she to build that bookstore?*

If any of those thoughts have swirled around in your head, I'm going to give you one shift that's going to change everything for you. *If not you, then who?*

If you aren't willing to take your brilliance and share it with this world, then who will? What if Noelle had never built that bookstore? What if she had never given her community a chance to discover new books and ideas, attend empowering author talks, and connect with other readers? My guess is that people would still be signing a petition that would ultimately go nowhere.

What if I had never written *Girl Code*? I think about that often. I wonder where so many of my readers would be if those ideas inside that book had not gotten into their hands. I wonder how many businesses would never have been launched, or how many women would still be stuck in their dead-end jobs.

What if I had never written this book?

Of course, I don't take full responsibility for the paths my readers choose. It takes a bad ass woman to take action upon inspiration. But I do realize I have been a part of their journeys. And knowing that is what keeps me focused on going even bigger – and showing them that they can do the same.

Have you ever been motivated to do something because of a book you read? Or a documentary you saw? Or something someone said to you? Those things that move us all originate from a source. And if that source had never taken a chance and put those ideas and words out there, then perhaps you wouldn't have been inspired to move.

There is a massive ripple effect that comes from our work. James Altucher suggests drawing a circle on a piece of paper, and inside that circle, writing down what it is you do. So, for example, mine might say, "I write books that empower women." Then he asks you to draw a circle around that circle, with the names of people you know your work has impacted. So, I might write down a few of my close friends or clients who have expressed to me that my books have deeply resonated with them. Next, he asks you to draw a circle around that circle, and write down the people who have been impacted by the people in the previous circle. You essentially keep drawing those circles, and soon you begin to see the massive impact you have on this world when you do what you do. It's a profound exercise and I highly recommend doing it.

Now, imagine you decide to keep playing small and never go for it? Think about the thousands, if not millions of people who would never be impacted by your work. My podcast, *Style Your Mind*, has 6 million unique downloads to date. That means 6 million individuals have heard my message. 6 million! If I had never asked myself, "Why not me?" then there is a possibility those 6 million lives wouldn't have been inspired to do great things. Even if 1/100th of those listeners took action based on the empowering words they hear through my podcast, that is a massive contribution to this world.

So, I'm going to ask you again – why not you? If you are blessed with a gift and a vision to bring that gift to life, then it is your responsibility to make it happen. Period, end of story. In fact, it's quite selfish to keep your gifts to yourself. Think about all the lives you could potentially touch if you could just get out of your own damn way.

Things change when you realize you're here for a bigger purpose. When you understand that you are a vessel, and that your small ego is just that – small. You are enough. You have everything it takes.

You are the girl on fire. And you're here to light up the world.

CONNECT WITH CARA

Listen to her podcast, *Style Your Mind*, on iTunes, Spotify, Google Play, or your favorite podcast app

Learn more about Cara at TheChampagneDiet.com

Follow her on Instagram @TheChampagneDiet

Made in the USA
Monee, IL
16 June 2023

c229a6d7-9c89-4a6c-84e1-927c11bbb538R01